Project Management

Other titles in the Briefcase Books series include:

To learn more about titles in the Briefcase Books series go to
www.briefcasebooks.com

Project Management

Second Edition

Gary R. Heerkens

Jew York Chicago San Francisco Athens
ondon Madrid Mexico City Milan New Delhi
ingapore Sydney Toronto

1 2 3 4 5 6 7 8 9 0 QFR/QFR 1 8 7 6 5 4 3

ISBN   978-0-07-181848-3
MHID   0-07-181848-0

e-ISBN   978-0-07-181852-0
e-MHID   0-07-181852-9

This is a CWL Publishing Enterprises book developed for McGraw-Hill by CWL Publishing Enterprises, Inc., Madison, Wisconsin, www.cwlpub.com.

McGraw-Hill Education products are available at special quantity discounts to use as premiums and sales promotions, or for use in corporate training programs. To contact a representative, please visit the Contact Us pages at mhprofessional.com.

Contents

Contents

Acknowledgments

The ideas and practices covered in this book are the result of countless discussions with project management professionals and many other associates willing to share their experiences, insights, and opinions. Unfortunately, I cannot list all of the people who helped me learn how to manage projects, or all of my friends and colleagues in the Project Management Institute who have helped to broaden my knowledge. But I do appreciate them nonetheless.

And I would be remiss if I did not acknowledge the contribution of the many students who have attended my seminars and were willing to discuss the problems and issues confronting them—they have provided some of the most valuable insights of all.

Introduction

I was thrilled when John Woods from CWL Publishing Enterprises asked me to write the second edition of this book, as it offered me an opportunity to introduce a whole new generation of readers of my book to an important project management concept: business savvy.

Project management is not known for revolutionary change, yet a subtle transformation has been taking place since the first edition was published. This transformation is nearly complete and can be expressed this way: project managers are now expected to be business-savvy. In addition to being proficient at the mechanics of project management (the primary focus of this book), today's project managers must also understand that projects are financial investments. This simple realization is described and explored in Chapter 4, a significant new addition to the second edition.

As in the first edition, this book chronicles the exploits of Brad—a fictional character who's been thrust into the world of project management. But this time, the expectations of Brad's capabilities have increased. This is indicative of another shift in the field of project management: project managers are expected to do more and to know more than in the past. Fortunately for Brad (and you!), the second edition offers a new level of sophistication with regard to the way he discovers the tools and techniques of project management.

The first three chapters lay out everything you need to know about projects, project management, and the role of project manager. Establishing a foundation of understanding in these areas will provide the context you need to better understand the world you and Brad are about to enter.

Chapter 4 describes the processes needed to ensure that only the most worthy projects are identified and selected. As mentioned above, this area addresses the business side of project management—and represents the greatest opportunity for personal and professional growth for all project managers.

Once the best projects are selected, it's time to execute them.

Achieving excellence in managing the execution of projects begins with a deep understanding of planning and estimating. This is the focus of Chapter 5.

Chapter 6 is devoted to the process of properly defining and launching your project. It addresses one of the most common (and costly) project management missteps in companies: solution-jumping. This chapter will equip you to excel, providing the tools, techniques, and insights needed to help your company get its projects headed in the right direction.

The ideas and tactics in Chapter 7 will help you sharpen your leadership skills. Even the most proficient project managers cannot accomplish their mission without the support of a team, and this chapter offers insights on how to get the most from your team while fostering relationships that will make them want to be part of any future projects you manage.

Chapter 8 shows you how to manage the environment that surrounds your project. Just like Brad, you will discover that there are a myriad of people and things trying to pull your project in different directions. In this chapter, you'll learn how to manage your project interfaces in an effective manner.

In Chapter 9, you will roll up your sleeves and develop an Integrated Project Plan. Expect a detailed exploration of tools and techniques in this chapter, as the methods described here will form the core of your project management skills.

One of the biggest single challenges all project managers face is risk and uncertainty. By their very nature, projects are one-time events. This means that you can't always be sure what to expect or know how things will turn out. Chapter 10 shows you how to address that challenge so as to, if not eliminate risk, manage it effectively.

Chapter 11 describes how you can stay in control while the project work is being done, even though there are many different people doing many different things. The key to tackling this challenge, as you will see, is information. And plenty of it.

Eventually, your project will come to an end. Brad discovered that this part of the project is surprisingly challenging. Confusion and chaos are not unlikely in the waning days of the project. Chapter 12 shows you how you can cut through this chaos and drive your project to a successful conclusion.

The first edition of this book got high marks for being realistic in the way it explored the challenges of project management. The second edition is even more realistic. You may find some comments and insights to be surprisingly revealing and direct. My mission was to offer advice that would provide you with the maximum possible value. This, at times, required me to "tell it like it is."

Special Features

Titles in the Briefcase Books series are designed to give you practical information written in a friendly, person-to-person style. The chapters deal with tactical issues and include lots of examples. They also feature numerous sidebars that give you different types of specific information. Here's a description of the sidebars you'll find in this book.

KEY TERM

Every subject has some jargon, including project management. The Key Term sidebars provide definitions of terms and concepts as they are introduced.

SMART

MANAGING

The Smart Managing sidebars do just what their name suggests: give you tips to intelligently apply the strategies and tactics described in this book to help you implement the projects you manage.

TRICKS OF THE TRADE

Tricks of the Trade sidebars give you insider how-to hints on techniques astute managers use to execute the tactics described in this book.

It's always useful to have examples that show how the principles in the book are applied. The For Example sidebars provide illustrations of how the ideas in this book have been successfully used by managers.

Caution sidebars warn you where things could go wrong when undertaking new projects.

How can you make sure you won't make a mistake when you're trying to implement the techniques the book describes? You can't, but the Mistake Proofing sidebars give you practical advice on how to minimize the risk of this happening.

The Tools sidebars provide specific directions for implementing the techniques described in the book in a systematic fashion.

Project Management

Congratulations! You're the Project Manager!

Brad picks up the phone before the second ring. It's his boss, Gina. "Brad, I'd like you to stop by my office right after lunch today."

Brad is not sure why the boss is calling him into her office, which makes for a long lunch hour. He knows he's been doing a good job lately. As a matter of fact, he knows that he's probably the most technically capable person in the group. "No, wait," he says to himself in a frenzy of self-doubt. "Maybe I did something I wasn't supposed to. Or maybe I didn't do something I should have?"

Countless positive and negative scenarios run through Brad's overworked mind until 1 o'clock finally rolls around. He apprehensively enters Gina's office.

"Brad, I've got some great news for you," Gina begins. "Since it's so closely related to what we do here, Project Apex has been assigned to our group." Brad smiles, not sure why.

Gina continues, "You're one of the best engineers I have." Brad's smile widens in anticipation. And then—without warning—Gina utters those fateful words. "Congratulations, Brad, I'm assigning you as the project manager for Project Apex."

Great news? Did she say *great* news? "What do I know about managing projects?" Brad wonders to himself.

As Brad turns to leave Gina's office, she delivers the knockout punch. "By the way, Brad," Gina says with a curious inflection in her voice, "I think you should be aware—management is *really* going to be watching this closely. There's an awful lot riding on the success of your project."

As Brad leaves Gina's office, the same two words keep ringing in his ears—*your project.*

The Accidental Project Manager

The story above is not an isolated anecdote. Every day, engineers, salespeople, technicians, and countless others are thrust into the role of project manager. They're very good at their current jobs. In fact, they're typically the most technically knowledgeable engineers or the most successful salespeople. Now they're about to become project managers.

KEY TERMS

Project "A temporary endeavor undertaken to create a unique product, service, or result," according to the Project Management Institute.

Project manager The person ultimately responsible for the success or failure of a project.

Accidental project manager A person who is placed into the role of project manager by organizational circumstance, rather than by design or voluntary choice of career path.

It's probably more appropriate to refer to them by their more popular (however informal) name—accidental project managers. An *accidental project manager* is a person who is placed into the role by organizational necessity and chance, rather than by design or choice of career path.

If you're an accidental project manager, one of the first things you should do is pause to consider whether you're cut out to be a project manager and determine whether it's what you really want to do. Why? Because if you do a reasonably good job leading your first project, chances are you'll be asked again. And again. And again. In other words, if you're finding yourself in the same position as Brad, you might be embarking on a new career. It would be wise to consider some of the pros and cons before saying yes to that career move.

The information, tools, and techniques presented in this book will move you well along in understanding the mechanics of managing proj-

THE PROS AND CONS OF BECOMING
A PROJECT MANAGER

CAUTION

Pros
- It can often be a stepping-stone to a promotion.
- It provides a strong sense of accomplishment.
- There's considerable variety; no two days are alike.
- There's significant freedom of choice.
- It affords the opportunity to effect change across the organization.

Cons
- It requires significant tolerance for politics.
- It requires significant tolerance for ambiguity and uncertainty.
- There's a lot of responsibility, but little or no authority.
- You may feel disconnected from your technical discipline.
- You may be perceived by some as not having "a real job."

ects. But it's important that you enter this new world with your eyes wide open. With that in mind, let's look closely at what you might expect to experience as a project manager.

What Might You Encounter Out There?

Although you won't often see it addressed in project management reference books, the reality is that mental preparedness may prove to be just as critical to your success as a project manager as your knowledge base or skill set. And gaining a sound understanding of what's involved in this new role is a critical step toward being mentally prepared. Let's explore those pros and cons by describing the life of a typical project manager—assuming there is such a thing as typical.

However Brad may feel about taking on his first project, the truth is that life as a project manager can be rewarding. You'll find it is different from almost any other job you've ever done. It's complex, varied, and interesting. If done well, it can lead to a strong sense of accomplishment. These are among the aspects that project managers identify as the main attractions to the job.

At the same time, however, being a project manager will test you in ways you cannot imagine now. You will become an organizational focal point. Everyone will look to you for the answers, but you must be careful not to try to provide all the answers; after all, that's why you have a team.

> **SMART MANAGING**
>
> **HANG IN THERE, BABY!**
> If you can get experienced project managers to let their guard down for a few moments, they'll probably admit that their first few projects didn't go very well—and that's the sugar-coated version. So be prepared for a rough start as you begin to manage projects. But if you hang in there, you'll find yourself rapidly moving through the learning curve. In the world of project management, experience is a particularly powerful and effective teacher.

And speaking of the team, one of the biggest shifts in behavior (and thinking) you'll encounter will be the need to rely on others to get things done. In most cases, that'll be your team. You'll quickly discover that there's far too much for you to do alone, yet delegation may prove to be a challenge for you. Empowering others, then trusting them to follow through, may be unsettling. You'll find yourself uncomfortable with the idea that others are doing things for which you will be held responsible.

You'll have lots of responsibility, but won't have the authority often perceived as being required to discharge that responsibility. You'll have to get things done through the people on your team without having any direct control over them. Among your most valuable tools will be the ability to persuade and influence, as you seek to mold a group of diverse personalities into a unified team with a commonality of purpose.

Not everyone on your team will be as knowledgeable and skilled as you would like. Nonetheless, you've got to get the job done using whatever resources have been provided. Project management lore is full of tales of project managers who were able to "take the hand that was dealt to them" and turn it into a successful project. For you to succeed, you'll have to rely on your ability to coach, mentor, and motivate to get the level of performance you need from those assigned to work on your project.

What kind of knowledge will you need to be a successful project manager? Well, you'll have to know a bit about almost everything. You'll have to pay attention to the details, but not get wrapped up in them. You'll have to make countless decisions with insufficient information and despite conflicting signals. You'll have to condition yourself to seek *acceptable* rather than *perfect* solutions. You'll have to blend technical expertise with a keen sense of human nature. You'll have to handle administrative matters.

And while you're busy doing your own thing, you'll have to cultivate and maintain a smooth working relationship with many other people, both inside and outside your organization. Unfortunately, as you seek to achieve the project goals, it's unlikely that everyone you encounter will be an ally. Organizational politics and reality dictate that not everyone will like project

> **UNCOVERING THE POTHOLES ON THE ROAD TO SUCCESS** SMART MANAGING
>
> Be proactive in determining who's likely to work with you and who's likely to work against you by arranging informal chats with key individuals in your organization. Initiate a casual discussion about the discipline of project management. In many cases, it won't take much time to figure out whether you can expect your relationship with that individual to be relatively smooth or rocky.

management or project managers (that's you!). Many people will admire your role, respect your position, and appreciate your involvement; others will not. You will need to figure out who's who between those two groups—fast.

But at the end of the project, you'll be able to look back and feel a deep sense of pride that comes with producing a successful outcome and creating positive change. Project leadership requires the use of many skill sets. It involves tasks of limitless variety. You must live by a curious combination of process compliance and individual judgment, of gut feelings and data, of people and things. The challenge is enormous.

So if you feel mentally prepared to accept this challenge, you're well on your way to becoming a successful project manager. The only thing left is to learn how to do it the right way.

Throughout this book, we tell you and show you how to do project management the right way. And although we focus primarily on the process, we never lose sight of the importance of the interpersonal aspects as well as the environmental aspects—the people and things that surround your project. Combined, the process and the people form the art and science of project management.

About the Art and Science of Project Management

Project management has two major aspects:

▪ the art—leading the people on the project and

▪ the science—defining and coordinating the work to be done.

The art of project management relates to the fact that projects are really about people getting things done. Project management requires a keen insight into human behavior and the ability to skillfully apply appropriate interpersonal skills.

The second aspect—and the focus of this book—involves the knowledge, understanding, and skillful application of a prescribed project management process. This process is intended to guide project managers and project teams to effectively perform key process steps, such as identifying the true need, defining the project objective, creating an execution schedule, and maintaining control throughout the project. The premise of the process is the development of a set of graphic tools, documents, and techniques, all aimed at facilitating project success. Among the graphic tools and documents are the Client Requirements Document, the Work Breakdown Structure, and the Network Diagram. Among the many techniques we cover is calculating net present value and preparing a comprehensive project proposal.

About This Book

As we focus on the tools and techniques of project management, we make a few key assumptions intended to represent the most common conditions for practicing project managers today. First, we assume that you are the person leading the project—irrespective of your position within the organizational hierarchy or your "real job." Second, we assume that you are managing projects within a *matrix environment.* This means that the project requires the efforts of individuals from a number of functional departments such as Marketing, Engineering, Human Resources, Operations, etc. Finally, we assume that you do not have direct control over these people; in other words, you are not their immediate supervisor. While this is not always the case, it is the most common situation in today's complex organizational environment.

However, even if you're not a practicing project manager or if you're a manager of project managers or an executive, this book can be of value to you. It can provide you with a wealth of knowledge and insight relative to the life of a project manager, enabling you to foster the support structure needed to help your project managers be successful. In fact, organizational managers play the key role in ensuring that a supportive environment is provided for project managers—like Brad.

Manager's Checklist for Chapter 1

☑ Project management is both an art and a science. The art is strongly tied to the interpersonal aspects—the business of leading people. The science (on which this book focuses) comprises an understanding of processes, tools, and techniques.

☑ All project managers are expected to be well versed in the science of project management. You cannot survive without being knowledgeable in this area.

☑ If you're an accidental project manager (put into the role rather than choosing it voluntarily), think about whether you're cut out to be a project manager before getting too involved. Although it can be personally satisfying, it's a tough job that requires a thick skin. If you do a good job, you'll probably be asked to lead more projects, so you'd better be OK with the role or your life will not be much fun.

☑ Generally speaking, the project manager's job is not intellectually challenging, but it is complex and broad. It requires a large variety of skills—many of which will be new to you.

An Overview of Projects and Project Management

Upon returning to his desk, Brad contemplates what lies ahead. Although a bit unnerved, he likes the idea of taking on a challenge.

"The visibility should help my career along," he says to himself with a smile, "as long as Project Apex turns out okay, that is." Brad's smile slowly turns into a slight frown. As he finishes the sandwich he was too nervous to eat before meeting with Gina, he decides to accept the assignment—though he's not sure he *really* has a choice!

Before tackling Project Apex, Brad realizes that he'd better do a quick study on project management—starting with the basics of what a project is and how project management is supposed to be done. He wants to be in the best possible position to make Project Apex a resounding success. Let's give him some help by examining project management from five perspectives:

1. The business perspective
2. The process perspective
3. The interpersonal and behavioral perspective
4. The organizational management perspective
5. Defining project success

Project Management: The Business Perspective

While the business aspect of a project is not generally viewed as a core element of project management methodology, it is nonetheless valuable for all project managers to keep one central point in mind: all projects are, at their core, *financial investments*. We explore the specific impact of this concept on projects in Chapter 4. But for now, let's discuss why you should care about the business perspective.

Project management is not known for undergoing revolutionary change. For the most part, much of what we cover in this book has been around for quite a while. What is changing within the profession of project management is this: organizations are growing more aware that they must pay much closer attention to the business side of projects. As an example, many organizations are starting to realize they must do a better job of aligning projects with corporate strategies and ensuring that the projects they pursue generate a positive cash flow. Actions such as this ensure that projects will contribute more to the bottom line and enable more efficient and effective use of resources—particularly human resources.

What does this mean for you, the project manager? It means that project business savvy—the knowledge of how the world of projects and the world of business are tied to one another—is rapidly becoming a sought-after competency. You are well advised to make business savvy a central focus of your professional development plan.

Project Management: The Process Perspective

Problems, needs, and opportunities continually arise in every organization. Problems like low operational efficiency, needs like additional office space, and opportunities like penetrating a new product market are but a few of the countless number of situations that managers must address in the course of operating an organization or company. Addressing these situations requires change. Projects are the vehicle for instituting change, and there's always someone responsible for guiding the successful completion of each project—the project manager. Project managers are change agents, and their road map for instituting change is the project management process.

What Is a Project?

Several definitions exist for *project*. We used a simple one in Chapter 1: "A temporary endeavor undertaken to create a unique product, service, or result." Despite how you choose to define the word, nearly every project you manage will have many of the same characteristics. Let's examine some of the most important ones.

A project is actually a *solution* to a problem, need, or opportunity. Further, it's a solution that *promises a benefit*. The benefit is normally tied to strategic or operational gains that result in some kind of financial benefit, such as an increase in revenue, a reduction in costs, or the avoidance of a negative economic impact. The benefits must outweigh the costs (called *financial justification*), which we explore in Chapter 4.

By definition, a *project* is temporary in nature; it has a specific start and finish. A project consists of a well-defined collection of small jobs (activities) and ordinarily culminates in the creation of one or more end products (deliverables). There will be a preferred execution sequence for the project's tasks (the schedule). Projects are ordinarily executed by a host organization and undertaken in service to a customer. The individuals or the organization that uses the project deliverables are users. A project is a unique, one-time undertaking; it will never again be done exactly the same way, by the same people, in the same environment. This is a noteworthy point, as it suggests that you may not have access to a wealth of historical information when you start your project. You'll have to launch your project with limited information or, worse, misinformation.

There will always be some uncertainty associated with your project. This uncertainty represents risk—an ever-present threat to your ability to make definitive plans and predict outcomes with high levels of confidence. All your projects will consume resources—resources in the form of time, money, materials, and human resources (people). One of your primary missions is to serve as the steward of these resources—to apply them as sparingly and as effectively as possible.

What Is Project Management?

A Guide to the Project Management Body of Knowledge (Project Management Institute, 2013) defines *project management* as "the application of knowledge, skills, tools and techniques to project activities to meet the project requirements." Although this definition may sound pretty straightforward, you will find that the skillful application of those skills, tools, and techniques will come only after you've had a significant amount of education and on-the-job experience.

The project management process calls for the creation of a small organizational structure (the project team), which is often a microcosm of the larger organization. Once the team has produced the desired outcome, the process calls for decommissioning that small organizational structure.

The Project Investment Life Cycle

This is the highest-level view of a project. This model is called the *project investment life cycle* because the collective goal of its component activities is to ensure the maximum benefit for the money invested in the project. Also called the *overall project life cycle*, this view takes into account all activities related to the project creation. Encompassing more than execution-related activities, it includes preproject activities as well as postproject activities (see Figure 2-1).

Preproject	Project Implementation	Postproject
■ Strategic planning	■ Project definition	■ Measure benefits realization
■ Operations planning	✓ clarify client requirements	■ Assess client readiness
■ Opportunity identification	✓ define project solution	■ Manage product life cycle
■ Project financial analysis	■ Project planning	■ Manage ongoing operations
■ Customer needs analysis	✓ scope of work	■ Develop maintenance plans
■ Business case preparation	✓ schedule	✓ service level agreements
■ Business risk assessments	✓ cost	■ Project management
■ Research and development	■ Project execution	✓ distribute lessons learned
■ Prototype testing	■ Project closeout	✓ update historical databases
■ Portfolio management		✓ update estimating models

Figure 2-1. Activities comprising the project investment life cycle

As the name suggests, preproject activities are done for the purpose of getting a project to the point of initiating a project implementation. Preproject activities describe the need for the project—and the value the project is expected to deliver to the host organization. It is the "business front end" of a project and answers two fundamental questions: Why do we need a project? What is the project's high-level business objective? We explore these types of questions in Chapter 4.

An important purpose of postproject activities is to verify and fully leverage all the benefits that a project promises to deliver. A closely related secondary purpose is to help the project customer (the user) get the maximum amount of utility and value from the project deliverables. Gaining an understanding of the postproject life cycle activities related to your project may be more important than you think. Your knowledge of the "how," "why," "when," and "where" of your project's deliverables will influence some of decisions you'll make during project implementation. Conversely, many decisions you make during project execution may have far-reaching and profound effects on the efficiency, productivity, utilization, and profitability of the project deliverables after the project has been completed.

Note that the center stage of this life cycle is the project implementation life cycle. Let's now look at that life cycle.

The Project Implementation Life Cycle

Many life cycle models that pertain to project execution (project implementation) comprise four phases, as Figure 2-2 illustrates.

Project Investment Life Cycle

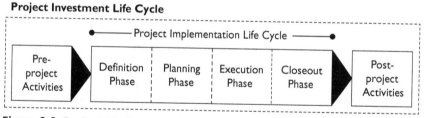

Figure 2-2. Project implementation life cycle

During the first of these four phases, the Definition Phase, the project is formally launched. The original problem, need, or opportunity is defined and quantified in detail. After conducting an alternatives analysis, an appropriate response is determined and defined in the form of a proposed solution. (An approved solution is actually "the project.") The major project deliverables are identified. The combination of the problem, solution, and major deliverables is often referred to as the *project scope*. The functional work groups needed to carry out the project are identified. Specific members of those work groups may be identified, marking the initial formation of a project core team.

Next is the Planning Phase, where the project solution is defined in greater detail. A strategy for delivering the project solution is developed in the form of an Integrated Project Plan. Developing a sound plan begins by defining the Required Work Elements (the scope of work, or project activities) and the optimum sequence for executing them (the project schedule). This enables estimates to be made relative to the amount of time needed to perform the work (the project duration) and how much money will be needed to fund the initiative (the project budget).

At this point, knowledge of the solution may prompt a question of technical feasibility (Can we do the project?). Initial estimates of project cost and schedule derived from project planning benefits may prompt an organization to revisit the question of financial justification (Should we do the project?) that was first raised during the preproject stage. It's generally good practice to address the feasibility and justification questions if you will be seeking formal management approval to proceed to the project execution phase, where the largest application of human resources (and money!) will occur.

During the third phase, the Execution Phase, the prescribed work is performed under the watchful eye of the project manager. Progress is continuously monitored, and appropriate adjustments are made and recorded as *variances* from the original plan. Throughout this phase, the

SMART

MANAGING

YOU CAN HELP!

While uncommon, some organizations try to execute projects without having a well-documented or formalized project management methodology in place. If your company lacks a methodology, this may represent an excellent opportunity for you. Seek out organizational managers who you believe are supportive of project management and suggest that they could leverage your expertise in developing a formal project management process manual. (Tip: Start with your boss!) This could help you in many ways. Your life as a project manager is likely to smooth out in an environment that recognizes and applies a widely adopted methodology for implementing projects. It may also offer you an opportunity for greater exposure through your interaction with management as you develop the methodology. Finally, you are likely to gain status by displaying initiative and helping your company evolve.

project team focuses on meeting the objectives developed and agreed on at the project outset.

During the final phase, the Closeout Phase, the emphasis is on verifying that the project has satisfied (or is expected to satisfy) the original need. Ideally, the project culminates with a smooth transition from deliverable creation (the project) to deliverable utilization (the postproject life cycle). The customer formally accepts the project deliverables. Throughout this final phase, project resources (the project team members) are gradually redeployed and the project shuts down. Although the project team and the project manager typically stop participating at this point, they can benefit greatly from understanding and appreciating what goes on after the project.

Project Management: The Interpersonal and Behavioral Perspective

Although this book focuses primarily on process, a full and fair treatment of project management would be incomplete without some discussion of the interpersonal and behavioral aspects of project management. You will find that the interpersonal and behavioral aspects of project life are crucial to a project's success. In fact, studies often point to interpersonal and behavioral problems as root causes for project failure. As mentioned previously, the art of project management is about dealing with people and about getting work done through other people. So let's take a look at the competency of project leadership.

The Immense Value of "Soft Skills"

Most projects require the efforts of a team of people. These people ordinarily possess a wide variety of skills, backgrounds, biases, work habits, values, and ethics—and may not be accustomed to working with one another. The project manager must have an ability to meld this diverse group of people into a single-minded and effective working unit.

Many project teams cut across organizational boundaries and include representatives from several departments or groups. Each representative brings a perspective or orientation influenced by his or her work group. Project managers must consider all these perspectives, while gently combining them into a singular perspective that considers the project mission—and project success—as the most important perspective for the duration of the team.

Project success depends on the cooperation of many people. Since most project managers are not granted the formal authority to literally direct others, they must rely on influence and persuasion to gain this cooperation.

In today's complex and varied organizational environments, human relations skills—the soft skills—are vital to success in project work. Project managers' skills in this area are integral to their role as project managers.

Creating a Motivating Environment

Beyond possessing the ability to influence and persuade the people on your team to produce the desired performance, you must also learn how to motivate them to keep them energized toward meeting goals. This is a controversial topic.

Can you truly motivate the individuals on your team? Many experts think not, primarily because motivation is viewed as an internal function. However, you certainly can (and should) create a climate, environment, or situation where motivation can occur within an individual. Motivation is all about recognizing a need that exists in an individual and finding a way to satisfy that need. This is a key point in understanding how to develop a high-performing team.

Managing Diverse Objectives and Perspectives

Sometimes, individual team members have their own objectives (some call it a hidden agenda) based on their personal situation, technical discipline, or feelings of allegiance toward their work group. Individual team members who have their own objectives can undercut team cohesion and weaken the team's dedication to the project. Allowing individuals too much freedom to pursue their own objectives can be counterproductive to fulfilling project objectives.

As your team comes together, be on the lookout for displays of individual objectives. For example, someone from the Marketing department may focus entirely on the optimization of product reliability, usefulness to the end user, or customer appeal. A representative of the Human Resources department may be driven solely by quality of work life issues

PRACTICAL TIPS FOR CREATING A MOTIVATIONAL CLIMATE

Tip #1: Convey the attitude that people and their work are valued.

- Take time to explain how each member's efforts contribute to project success.
- Take time at team meetings to highlight the specific contributions of the members.
- Heighten the exposure of low visibility or underappreciated responsibilities.

Tip #2: Convey confidence in people's knowledge, ability, and work ethic.

- Avoid double-checking and micromanagement as much as possible.
- Assign goals that represent a stretch for the individual, then let him or her determine how best to achieve those goals.
- Provide freedom, decision-making power, and authority in a way that conveys trust.

Tip #3: Recognize good performance.

- Clarify in advance what represents a high standard of performance.
- Communicate achievements of your team to management in a visible and positive way.
- Openly recognize attempts to go beyond what's expected.

Tip #4: Lead by example.

- Don't ask others to do things that you would not be willing to do yourself.
- Intercede on behalf of team members when warranted.
- Maintain the highest levels of honesty and integrity at all times.

or workforce morale. These are certainly noble causes, but they must be considered along with other factors in the context of the overall project mission. At times, personal agendas—such as ambition with intent for personal gain at all costs—create challenging situations for you as the project manager. You must learn to recognize and discourage all kinds of personal objectives and to focus the entire team on the overall project objectives.

Project managers may also have to manage the diverse objectives of individuals and groups outside the project team, such as suppliers, subcontractors, and partners. Members of these groups will often have parochial—often self-serving—perspectives. Getting them to rally behind your project's objectives instead of their own can be challenging at times.

Finally, in today's global environment, managing diverse objectives may apply to issues of culture, politics, and customs. For some, affiliation with other members of a team offers an opportunity to promote their own interests, beliefs, opinions, or causes. This can be tricky, as you must value diversity among your team members, but not allow it to distract from your project.

Project Management: The Organizational Management Perspective

Life as a project manager in a complex organization offers many challenges. The people on your project team come from different functional work groups, which creates leadership challenges for you. Your organization's management is likely to have an opinion on the value of project management methods. You need to clearly understand that perspective and what it means to you. And overall, your entire organization is currently operating at some level of project management excellence—or maturity.

These and other aspects of organizational life serve as the backdrop as you seek to discharge your responsibilities as project manager. How well you understand and adapt to these aspects is what determines your political savvy—a key component of your functional competency. Let's explore these organizational issues.

Overcoming the Silo Mentality

This issue is tied to our earlier discussion on personal objectives. Project core teams comprise representatives from a variety of work groups, as a variety of skill sets is required to execute projects effectively. It is not uncommon for individuals' viewpoints to align with their discipline or work group. Carrying this perspective too far, however, results in a phenomenon called *silo mentality*.

The challenge for you is to ensure that team members are always thinking about what's best for the project, not what's best for their professional discipline or their organizational department. Coach them, for example, to refrain from making decisions that optimize their specific aspect of the project until they've verified that someone else's part—or that the overall project—will not be adversely affected. (Obviously, this is easier said than done!)

One of the best ways to get team members to work across functional lines is by driving commonality in the application of project management tools and techniques. Project management methodology should be the glue that binds your "temporary organization" together. You must tirelessly promote the idea that every team member must focus on what's best for the project.

Silo mentality This is defined as when an individual places the needs, interests, and goals of his or her **KEY TERM** own department or work group ahead of the project's needs, interests, and goals, to the detriment of that project. Also known as *silo thinking*, this term is derived from how organizational charts are normally depicted. Team members who think exclusively in terms of their own department or work group are said to be thinking vertically (in *functional silos*), rather than considering what's best across the entire project (*horizontal thinking*).

How Does Upper Management View Projects?

Traditionally, projects have been viewed as rooted in technology, as the core objective of many projects is oriented toward delivering technology solutions. Unfortunately, this orientation has obscured the true purpose of projects. The truth is that projects are all about business—not technology.

The fundamental objective of a project is to achieve a business result, such as improving effectiveness, increasing sales, or making operations more efficient. That should be management's orientation.

This topic can also have significant implications for the project management process. For example, organizations should place a strong emphasis on process steps such as preparing a project business case. Business cases display anticipated project expenditures versus savings, cost-benefit ratios, and the anticipated business impact on the organization.

It makes a great deal of sense to ask project management practitioners to participate in the development of project business cases—yet this is rarely done.

Why? (Hint: See above!) It's because many organizational managers still view project management as a technical discipline, not a business

SMART

MANAGING

HELP YOURSELF (AND YOUR ORGANIZATION) BY BECOMING MORE PROJECT BUSINESS SAVVY

To help your organization evolve and take project management to the next level, seize any and all opportunities to enlighten your organizational managers on the fact that projects are really financial investments. You can also help the cause by ensuring that your competencies extend beyond your functional and technological knowledge and skills. Expand your understanding of how business methods, business strategies, and business skills are related to project work. Finally, adopt an entrepreneurial spirit in the way you execute your projects. Manage your project as if you were a businessperson starting up a small enterprise. Your project will have a better chance to generate positive business results. And after all, that is the point, isn't it?

discipline! You can help project management evolve by changing this perception.

Your Organization's Project Management Maturity

The project management maturity of your organization has a significant effect on how the project management discipline is carried out and what your life as a project manager will be like. Several models exist for evaluating an organization's project management maturity, and most identify five levels of maturity. Whatever process is used to describe maturity, the metrics usually evaluate:

- The extent to which project process documentation has been developed and distributed
- How well the project management process is understood throughout the organization
- The ability of the project team to predict outcomes with reasonable accuracy
- The efficiency with which projects are executed
- The perceived success rate of projects
- The organization's ability to learn from its experiences
- The extent of continuous improvement in project processes over time

The combination of your organization's project management maturity and your management's opinion of the value, purpose, and function of project management will often dictate the boundaries of your authority and responsibilities as a project manager.

Other Dynamics of Managing Projects in Organizations

Project managers often face a "two-dimensional" challenge related to organizational structure—cross-functional departments overlaid onto hierarchical authority. Many functionally based hierarchies have rules governing matters such as who should (or can) make certain decisions, who should (or can) direct the efforts of others, and how people should communicate.

For example, your organization may have a formal communication process in place that prescribes how information is to be transferred between heads of departments. This kind of formality would ordinarily require information and data to move up and down—within, as well as across, multiple organizations. Savvy project managers will appreciate that this mode of operation may considerably slow down communication, so they may choose to leverage informal communication channels to move information more quickly.

A company's organizational structure may also influence certain project leadership practices. In a purely *functional organization*, decision making and authority rest primarily in the hands of functional departments. This can make your life tough, because the authority of project managers is minimal, if nonexistent. At the other end of this continuum lies the *projectized organization*, where project managers have tremendous influence, authority, and decision-making power. These are typically organizations whose core business is executing projects, such as large consulting firms and contracting companies. Most organizations are somewhere between these extremes. In these *matrix organizations*, the decision making and the authority are shared between project managers and functional management. As a project manager, you need to understand where your organization falls along this continuum and use this as a basis for determining your limits of authority and participation in the decision-making processes.

Defining Project Success

The definition of *project success* is obviously critical, because in part, that's how you'll be judged as a project manager. You can define project success in many ways. To add to the confusion, every organization has its own view of what matters in project outcomes.

You're probably aware of a popular definition of success: the so-called "triple constraint" (cost, schedule, and sometimes scope). This definition has two significant drawbacks: (1) while most triple constraint models identify cost and schedule as two of the success dimensions, there are differing views on what the third dimension ought to be; and (2) it is a narrow and limiting interpretation of success.

So, instead of trying to focus on a single definition (like the triple constraints), let's consider project success in terms of a framework of thought.

If you think of the many ways that projects could be deemed successful, you come to realize that project success actually exists on several levels—each with a unique perspective and set of metrics. And despite the specific values used to quantify success or failure, the principles remain constant. Figure 2-3 shows a framework that identifies five levels of project success.

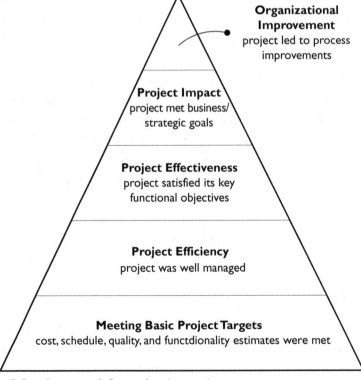

Figure 2-3. A framework for evaluating project success

Level 1: Meeting Basic Project Targets

Did the project meet the original targets of cost, schedule, quality, and functionality? Although it may seem admirable to beat these targets (i.e., finish under budget), success at Level 1 should actually measure whether the project manager did what was expected. In other words, maximum success would be defined as zero variance between the forecasted project targets and actual results. There are at least two reasons why this interpretation makes sense: first, it provides the certainty that organizational managers need to run the business; and second, project managers who always beat targets are suspect—they may be underestimating as a way to make their results look good.

Level 2: Project Efficiency

How well was the project managed? This is a metric for the process. If the project meets its targets, but the customer groups, project team, or others were adversely affected by the project experience, the project will not be perceived as successful. Project efficiency can be evaluated through the use of criteria such as these:

- The degree of disruption to the client's operation
- How effectively resources were applied
- The amount of growth and development of project team members
- How effectively conflict was managed
- The cost of the project management function

Level 3: Project Effectiveness

To what extent did the project fulfill its functional mission of solving a problem, exploiting an opportunity, or satisfying a need? Projects that do not satisfy the true need (or address the root cause) should rightfully be viewed as failures.

Here are some questions to help assess Level 3 success:

- Was the original problem solved?
- Is the customer using the product as intended?
- Has customer/user satisfaction been confirmed?

Level 4: Project Impact

Did the project investment meet its strategic, operational, and financial goals? This success metric asks critical questions such as:

- Was there a verifiable increase in revenue, profit, or sales?
- Did you save as much money as expected?
- Is the customer/user likely to do business with you again?

Level 5: Organizational Improvement

Did the organization learn from the project? Is that knowledge going to improve the chances that future projects will succeed at each of the four levels described above? High-performing organizations learn from their failures—and their successes—and use that knowledge to improve their success rate over time. This level assumes a long-term perspective and measures organizational learning and a resultant increase in project successes. The primary tools for organizational improvement are the maintenance of accurate historical records and the widespread use of lessons learned.

It's important to note that—as the levels get higher—the direct control that the average project manager can exert is likely to diminish. However, top-performing project managers still pay attention to all five success metrics and seek any opportunity to ensure their fulfillment.

Manager's Checklist for Chapter 2

☑ Projects possess several key characteristics. They are financial investments. They are temporary and unique. Their implementation comprises several activities that have a preferred sequence. Projects consume resources and result in products called *deliverables*. They ordinarily involve high levels of risk and uncertainty. Their objective is to produce strategic, operational, and financial benefits.

☑ These and other characteristics make projects different from day-to-day work; projects therefore call for the application of special management techniques.

☑ There are two ways to look at the life cycle of projects: (1) the project investment life cycle is a high-level, business-centric perspective of a project, (2) the project implementation life cycle is a component of the larger investment life cycle and focuses on the detailed definition, planning, and execution of the core project effort.

☑ Project implementation is carried out in four stages: *Definition*, where the project is defined and launched; *Planning*, where the solution is detailed and the work required to carry it out is identified and scheduled; *Execution*, where the work is done and monitored; and *Closeout*, where the project is brought to successful closure.

☑ Although you should follow a prescribed process to implement your project, your day-to-day decisions should also reflect project investment life cycle considerations. For example, you should be familiar with the benefits that your project is expected to deliver, and you should know exactly how your customer will use the project deliverables after the project is handed over.

☑ Most project managers work in complex organizations, where people who work on the team may come from several work groups. This can create unique management challenges for you, as you strive to get everyone to focus on doing what's best for the project.

☑ Project success exists on five levels: (1) Did the project meet the original targets of cost, schedule, quality, and functionality? (2) How well was the project managed? (3) To what extent did the project fulfill its functional mission of solving a problem, exploiting an opportunity, or satisfying a need? (4) Did the overall project investment meet its strategic, operational, and financial goals? (5) Did the organization learn from the project?

About the Role of Project Manager

A s we mentioned in Chapter 1, the project manager's job is diverse—as a matter of fact, you're supposed to make it that way! Among the most useful pieces of advice we can offer for success as a project manager is to "think like a generalist." This means avoiding the natural tendency to devote too much of your attention to those aspects of the project that are familiar and comfortable. This is only one of the many challenges you can expect to face as you assume the project manager mantle. In this chapter, we take a look at your role from a variety of perspectives.

The Inherent Responsibilities of a Project Manager

The responsibilities inherent to the role of project manager fall into four broad areas:

1. Your project
2. Your organization (and your management)
3. Your team
4. Yourself

Each area of responsibility has a slightly different focus, adding to the diversity of the role.

The most obvious and the largest responsibility is the one you have to the project. You're expected to meet the cost, schedule, functionality, and quality targets. You must run the project efficiently. You must act as an arbiter for the differing objectives that will inevitably exist within and across the team, as discussed in Chapter 2.

You also have a responsibility to your organization and your management. The project you're managing is expected to provide a tangible return to your organization. We discuss the extent to which you're held responsible for guaranteeing this return in Chapter 4. You're viewed as an "agent" of your organization and its management. You're expected to adhere to the organization's policies and act within the limits of authority granted to the project manager's role. You're expected to make decisions in the best interests of the organization—which may be challenging at times, as decisions that benefit your organization are not always the best ones for the project.

Yet another responsibility you have to your organization relates to the information flow. This includes honest estimating, timely status reporting, and accurate forecasting. Proactively keeping management informed of project status and forecasts—good or bad—is one of your more important

> **TRICKS OF THE TRADE**
>
> ### DISCOVERING WHAT YOUR ORGANIZATION EXPECTS
>
> It's smart to understand what your organization expects of you as a project manager. As with other types of organizational expectations, talk with your peers. Sometimes what's in your organization's documented procedures doesn't accurately reflect reality. When it comes to understanding your organization's expectations, experienced project managers have discovered that the documented procedures (what is stated as desirable in the process manual) may not be as reliable an indicator as organizational behavior (what actually gets rewarded).

responsibilities as a project manager, perhaps even critical to your survival. The key word here is *proactively*. You are responsible for preventing management from being unpleasantly surprised.

You are expected to offer your management appropriate opportunities to intercede in guiding the course of your project.

The responsibilities you have to your team will vary from project to project and team to team. These responsibilities include ensuring that the team is properly informed throughout the project, providing constructive feedback when warranted, and giving positive, fair, and appropriate recognition for performance. These responsibilities are not easy. One of your biggest challenges will be striking the right balance among the needs of the individual team members, the needs of your team as a unit, and the needs of your project. Superior project managers further accept the informal responsibility for providing growth and development opportunities for individual team members whenever possible.

Your final responsibility is to yourself. Though not often discussed in project management textbooks, this responsibility is vital—particularly if you view project management as your chosen profession. The odds are that your organization still does not have well-developed career paths and career development programs geared specifically to project management as a discipline. If you're fortunate enough to have this support, congratulations! If not, then the responsibility for your personal growth and development falls largely on you. Later in this chapter, we explore the roles of introspection and self-awareness in this process.

Common Challenges You Can Expect to Face

As mentioned previously, expect to face many challenges as you take on the responsibility of managing a project in your organization. Whatever the specifics of your particular situation, many of the challenges you'll face are faced by most project managers. Let's review a few of these common challenges.

The Responsibility-Versus-Authority Trap

Firmly embedded in project management folklore is this one: the responsibility you've been given is not commensurate with the authority (or formal power) you believe you need to accomplish the mission. The size of the gap between responsibility and authority partially depends on your organization's structure. If you're in a purely functional organization—and in many cases, a matrix organization—you should not expect to be granted much formal authority. The gap between responsibility and authority is wide. To compensate for your perceived lack of formal authority, you have to rely on *expert power* (respect you can garner through superior knowledge or capability) or *referent power* (often acquired by practicing an excellent leadership style). You'll also need to rely heavily on your ability to influence and persuade.

Imposition of Unrealistic Targets

Sound project management practice suggests that project goals (cost, schedule, quality, and functionality) should be determined through a systematic process of understanding customer needs, identifying the best solution, and formal planning. Throughout a project, realistic assumptions about resource availability, quality of materials, and work processes (just to name a few factors) should be used. This approach yields a credible estimation of what is reasonably achievable. If this estimation does not meet business goals, then a systematic risk-versus-return process should be pursued until it can be verified that the targets are achievable within a given level of elevated risk.

That's the process that *should* be followed.

Unfortunately, far too many project managers work in a world where project targets are based on what management or a customer wants or needs, rather than what is feasible. In many cases, targets are developed before it's even known what the project effort entails! When this happens, a struggle begins, as the team tries to force the project to fit within the boundaries that have been drawn.

REVERSE SCHEDULING

If you've been assigned to a project with an imposed end date, avoid the temptation to develop your schedule by starting with the finish date and working your way back to the current date. This creates a false sense of what's achievable and masks the true level of risk involved in meeting that date. Refer to Chapter 10 for more on this topic.

This practice puts project managers in a difficult position, as it sets them up for failure and undermines the planning process. Unfortunately, this phenomenon seems to have reached epidemic proportions: it's one of the biggest complaints of practicing project managers today.

Emphasis on Departments Versus Projects

If you're managing a project in a matrixed organization, one of the more difficult challenges you'll face is getting team members to overcome their inherent tendency to think and act in terms of optimizing their own discipline, profession, technical field, department, or work group. Recognize that this phenomenon is fueled by three powerful influences. First, by definition, projects are temporary, but an individual's core function lives on. In other words, a person often considers his or her work group to be "home"; the project is only a passing state of existence. Second, unless contemplating a formal career change to project management, a person considers his or her discipline, area of expertise, or profession as his or her primary work focus—after all, it's what the company hired the person to do. This means that he or she will likely be strongly committed to ensuring the well-being of that area. Finally, there's the power of the paycheck. Simply stated, most people align their loyalties with the source of their paycheck. Ordinarily, that's their work group or functional department, not you.

The Dual-Responsibility Trap

Most project managers are asked to wear two hats. They must perform their job duties while acting as the project manager. (Brad from Chapter 1 is in that position, working as senior technical lead and managing Project Apex.) This situation presents additional challenges for you.

At the center of this dilemma is the issue of allegiance. Imagine for a moment that you're facing a critical decision. Unfortunately, what's best for the project will negatively impact your work group, but what benefits your work group will hurt your project. What's the right decision? What do you do? If you decide in favor of your work group, you risk being viewed as a poor project manager. If you choose the opposite course of action, you may incur the wrath of your peers and/or departmental management. It's a tough spot—and you can almost bank on being in it, possibly often.

A more fundamental problem of the dual responsibility trap is figuring out how to divide your time and attention between the roles. How much should you allocate to each? How long can you satisfy both before you realize you're working most nights and weekends?

A third issue may surface in the form of the "two-boss syndrome." The project manager reports to his or her functional supervisor and to the person in charge of the organization's project management function. Again, this is a difficult situation for most project managers.

The Conflict of Certainty and Uncertainty

Among the biggest challenges in project work is the fundamental disconnect between the certainty that organizational managers need to properly run the business and the inherent uncertainty of project work.

For example, suppose you're just beginning a project. Many unknowns lie ahead, and you're faced with a great deal of uncertainty. In this kind of situation, good project management practice suggests that you should express project estimates (such as the final project cost and completion date) as a "ranged estimate" of possible outcomes, rather than a so-called "point estimate." The size of your range should reflect the extent of your knowledge of project details and the amount of uncertainty you are facing. And so it may be appropriate to estimate that the final cost of your project will be "between $425,000 and $500,000."

KEY TERMS   **Point estimate** This refers to any project result (completion date, cost expenditure, or deliverable performance, for example) that is expressed as a specific, single value. For example, predicting that "the project will be completed on October 19."

Ranged estimate This refers to a prediction that uses an upper and lower limit. For example, predicting that "the project will be completed sometime between October 7 and October 29." The size of the range should reflect the extent of unknowns and uncertainty. Using ranged estimates offers an excellent way for a project manager to convey the existence of uncertainty.

Many project managers today would receive an unfavorable response from their management to that type of "crude" estimate. It doesn't provide the certainty that management requires for approval. (To be blunt, it also reflects a lack of understanding on the part of management about the amount of risk and uncertainty inherent in project work.)

Unfortunately, this example is not exceptional. The uncertainty associated with projects exists throughout the life of the project. It simply never goes away—nor does management's craving for certainty.

Skill Requirements of the Project Manager

To fulfill the responsibilities described above and handle the challenges you'll face, you'll need to possess a wealth of knowledge and a diverse set

HELP YOURSELF BY EDUCATING OTHERS   SMART

You can expect to encounter many people who don't understand the finer points of project management, such as the use of ranged estimates in the face of uncertainty or the need to use influence to get things done due to a lack of formal authority. This is par-   **MANAGING** ticularly true in organizations that are only beginning to use formalized project management or have traditionally relied on a functional management approach. When you observe a "knowledge gap," taking the time to educate others about projects and project management will benefit you, as they begin to better understand your role and the nature of projects.

of skills. So what knowledge and skills does it take to be an effective project manager?

There are many ways to slice this pie. The way that makes the most sense to me is to break it down into four major knowledge and skill categories:

1. Project management process skills
2. Interpersonal and behavioral skills
3. Technology management skills
4. Desired personal traits

Let's examine each one.

Project Management Process Skills

Sometimes called the "hard skills," this set of capabilities relates to the mechanics of project management. You should be very knowledgeable of the project management process, which comprises a number of tools and techniques. For example, you should be able to prepare a comprehensive Customer Requirements document, develop a Network Diagram, and construct a Work Breakdown Structure.

Without these "hard skills," you'll find it difficult to coordinate and facilitate the creation of a high-quality project plan and to maintain control during project execution. Also, since these skills are a basic expectation, you can expect to encounter problems of respect from your team members if you're deficient in this area. This skill set is the main focus of this book.

Technology Management Skills

Most projects have one or more embedded technologies. An *embedded technology* refers to the process or technology areas at the core of the project. Examples might include software development, chemical processing, or commercial construction. Your ability to guide and coordinate the application of these technologies is crucial to your success. If you're like Brad in Chapter 1, you'll probably have sufficient knowledge and skills in the primary embedded technology of the project. However, it's likely that there will be several technology areas associated with your project. Although they will differ in focus, the process steps and related skills involved in managing their successful application will be similar.

Examples of technology management skills include:

- Proficiency in the project's core (primary) technology
- Proficiency in supporting technology areas
- General knowledge of your industry
- Ability to prepare comprehensive technical specifications
- Design skills
- Product knowledge
- Process knowledge
- Management of intellectual property

Interpersonal and Behavioral Skills

Since managing projects is all about getting things done through other people, your skills in dealing with people are of immeasurable value. Closely tied to your interpersonal skills are your behavioral skills: your personal conduct, style, and approach. Together, these two skill sets are often called the "soft skills." Here are some examples of soft skills:

- Relationship-building
- Conflict resolution
- Negotiation
- Influencing
- Delegating
- Coaching and mentoring

For individuals coming to project management from a highly technical background, soft skill development can be particularly challenging. Later in this chapter, we discuss ways to develop these skills.

> **MANAGING SUPPORTING TECHNOLOGIES**
> Your biggest challenge in the area of technology management
> will probably come from dealing with the people responsible **CAUTION**
> for managing the technology areas that lie beyond your own.
> It's likely that these people are your peers, which could lead to
> some angst, jealousy, or competition. Expect this interaction to test your
> interpersonal and behavioral skills as much as any other, perhaps more.

Desired Personal Traits

Closely related to soft skills are personal traits. Many studies have correlated personality traits to project management success. Although each
study reveals slightly different results, the traits shown in the following
list are those that appear most consistently.

- Honesty and integrity
- Ability to thinks like a generalist
- High tolerance for ambiguity
- High tolerance for uncertainty
- Persuasiveness
- Assertiveness
- Persistence
- Process-oriented thinking
- Self-awareness/reflectivity
- Openness and accessibility
- Political astuteness
- Decisiveness

Of the traits listed, the following are probably the most critical.

Ability to think like a generalist. Project managers must always be thinking in terms of the big picture. This can be a challenge for those accustomed to focusing more narrowly. Although this trait certainly requires
knowledge in many areas, what's crucial is that you pay attention and
care about everything and everybody.

High tolerance for ambiguity. You'll often receive mixed signals or contra-
dictory data. You need to develop processes—and the mental tough-
ness—for uncovering the truth and narrowing the inputs without getting
frustrated. This is not easy.

High tolerance for uncertainty. As with ambiguity, this is particularly challenging if you're entering project management from the technical arena and you're accustomed to working in an environment built on precision and reliable data. As a project manager, you must learn how to make decisions in the absence of complete information. And you must resign yourself to making decisions that are acceptable, yet not necessarily perfect.

Honesty and integrity. Although obvious virtues, these traits are worthy of specific mention. Studies routinely find that among the traits people most admire or desire in leaders, honesty and integrity *always* rise to the top. As a project manager, being referred to as "someone who does what she says she's going to do" is among the best accolades you can receive. Closely related is the issue of ethical behavior—having a reputation as someone who will stick to her or his principles, even in the face of adversity or temptation.

Together, the combination of hard skills, soft skills, functional competencies, and personal traits comprise the raw material for your capability as a project manager. But how do you develop that capability?

As Figure 3-1 reveals, skills that are mechanical in nature can be learned or developed through self-study, reading, or facilitated training

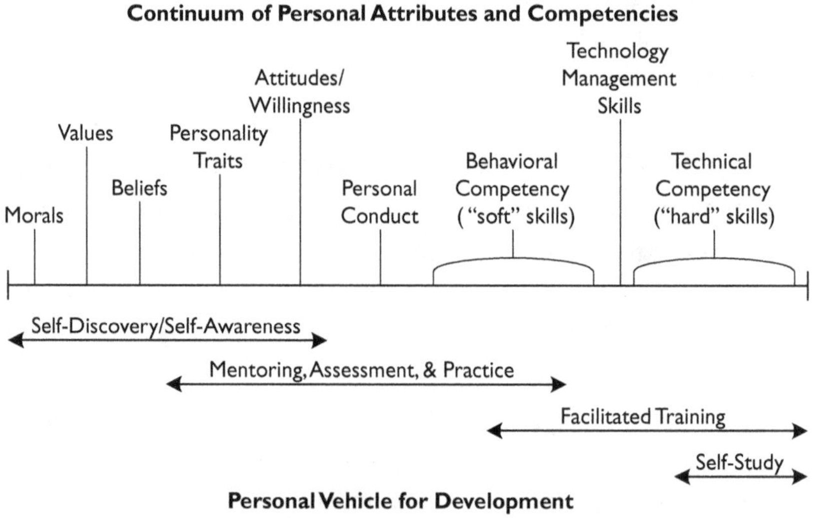

Figure 3-1. Personal attributes and their development

and practice. Many project management hard skills fall into this category. However, as you move into the soft skills, the preferred mode of development moves to coaching and mentoring. Here, soft skills are best developed through observation and feedback. Still further to the left are personality traits. And at the far left are traits that make up your personality and affect your behavior on a basic level. Here, the prospect of self-improvement is personal, and it's likely that you can only develop and improve through introspection—self-examination and self-analysis. The importance of introspection is discussed later in this chapter.

Functional Competencies of the Project Manager

Functional competencies refers to your ability to combine knowledge with skills and to apply them appropriately. Even if you're proficient in certain skill areas, your capability as a project manager is limited if you can't effectively apply those skills in day-to-day project duties. The shaded box contains a partial list of functional competencies.

PARTIAL LIST OF FUNCTIONAL COMPETENCIES FOR A PROJECT MANAGER

Project Management Process Functions

- Coordinates development of comprehensive, realistic, and understandable plans, estimates, and budgets
- Balances technical solutions with business and interpersonal factors
- Obtains formal approvals of project goals (cost, schedule, etc.) as needed
- Monitors progress and manages deviations in a timely, effective way
- Anticipates problems and reacts to change through a well-defined process

Technology Management Functions

- Ensures that a rational process is used to select the right technology
- Balances technology needs with the need to achieve business results
- Ensures appropriate technical disciplines are represented on the project
- Can assess the quality of technical decisions and recommendations
- Able to communicate technical information to a broad audience

Cognitive Functions

- Gathers information systematically; seeks input from several sources
- Collects the appropriate quantity of data before making a decision
- Draws accurate conclusions from quantitative data

- Makes decisions in an unbiased, objective manner using an appropriate process
- Understands the concept of risk versus return and makes judgments accordingly

Team Leadership Functions
- Fosters development of a common mission and vision
- Clearly defines roles, responsibilities, and performance expectations
- Uses a leadership style appropriate to the situation or stage of team development
- Fosters collaboration among team members
- Provides clear direction and priorities
- Removes obstacles that impede team progress, readiness, or effectiveness
- Promotes team participation in problem solving and decision making
- Passes credit on to the team; enables positive visibility to management
- Appreciates, promotes, and leverages the diversity within the team

Interpersonal Relationship Functions
- Communicates effectively with all levels in and out of the organization
- Negotiates fairly and effectively
- Brings conflict into the open and manages it collaboratively and productively
- Able to influence without relying on coercive power or threats
- Conveys ideas and information clearly and concisely, both in writing and verbally

Self-Management Functions
- Maintains focus and control when faced with ambiguity and uncertainty
- Shows consistency among principles, values, and behavior
- Tenacious in the face of pressure, opposition, constraints, or adversity
- Implements effectively; recognized as someone who "gets things done"
- Actively seeks feedback and modifies approaches accordingly

Motivational and Personal Development Functions
- Considers individual's skills, values, and interests when assigning tasks
- Allows team members an appropriate amount of freedom to do the job
- Accurately assesses individuals' strengths and development needs
- Continually seeks and offers opportunities for personal and professional growth
- Passes credit on to individuals; promotes their visibility to upper management
- Considers what drives an individual's behavior before trying to modify it
- Gives timely, specific, and constructive feedback

Customer Awareness Functions
- Anticipates customers' needs and proactively strives to satisfy them

- Accurately translates customers' verbalized wants into what they actually need
- Strives to understand customers and their business
- Responsive to customers' issues, concerns, and queries
- Actively strives to exceed customer expectations

Organizational Savvy Functions
- Involves the right people at the right time
- Understands and properly utilizes power and influence relationships
- Builds and leverages formal and informal networks to get things done
- Knows the mission, structure, and functions of the organization and others
- Understands profitability and general management philosophy
- Understands how project management is regarded by the organization
- Balances interests and needs of team/project with those of the broader organization

The Project Manager's "Unofficial" Job Duties

The functional competencies listed in the box above represent the official duties of the typical project manager. If your organization has developed a job description for project managers, it probably includes many of these functional competencies. What you won't find in job descriptions are the unofficial duties that project managers perform in the course of carrying out their mission. Let's examine some of the key unspoken competencies (somewhat tongue-in-cheek).

Babysitter. This refers to the need to provide close guidance or detailed instructions to certain individuals. This situation results from any number of causes. The person may be underqualified, lack confidence, or simply crave attention.

Salesperson. At times you'll have to rely heavily on your ability to influence others to sell an idea, a project, or yourself. Most selling situations are necessary and yield positive outcomes. However, if you find yourself spending too much time selling the project management discipline, that usually indicates a lack of understanding of or appreciation for the value of project management. Consider this an opportunity for education. (If, after a long time—say two years or so—the prevailing opinions of project management are still low, you may want to consider moving on.)

Teacher. This unofficial role often yields positive results. In fact, superior project managers educate and develop those they work with as they manage the project. Apply this skill, and you will tend to get the best people asking to be on your team.

Friend. Simultaneously maintaining friendships and professional relationships with people is difficult. However, if you can do it, you'll benefit greatly. In Chapter 2, we discussed the value of the informal communication network. An open, informal, and comfortable communication linkage is more likely to keep you supplied with more of the information you need than formal, rigorous, and stiff team meetings. Avoid the trap of believing that because you've been put in charge of a project you've risen above your peers and friendships no longer matter. Big mistake!

TRICKS OF THE TRADE

EIGHT KEY TIPS FOR SUCCESS AS A PROJECT MANAGER
People sometimes ask: What are the most valuable tips for becoming a superior project manager? There are numerous elements that contribute to success as a project manager, but here's a good start . . .

- Care about everything, and do not dwell on any one thing.
- Don't wait to be told to do something.
- Develop a keen understanding of human nature.
- Learn the "who, when, and how" of relying on others.
- Consider technology, people, process, and business when making decisions.
- Learn to make decisions with only ambiguous or incomplete information.
- Never stop developing your social skills.
- Appreciate the value of being politically savvy.

The Value of Introspection and Self-Awareness

To become a top-notch project manager, you must accept personal responsibility for your personal and professional growth and development—particularly in the areas of beliefs, values, and some personality traits—the softest of the soft skills (see list on page 35). Some project managers mistakenly believe that they can count on receiving a continuous stream of feedback on their performance and behavior because they are surrounded by others. This is not true.

Why not? Let's consider the groups of project players who surround you and the likelihood of getting high-quality feedback from them.

Project team members. Although I've stated that you don't have formal authority over team members, they will sense that you have some control over their destiny. Because they do not wish to jeopardize that, your chances of receiving negative feedback (which could be of great value to you) are pretty slim.

Customers. Most customers do not know much about your day-to-day conduct. Their opinions tend to be based more on outputs than competence (which is where you really need feedback). In addition, your relationship with clients tends to be artificial. Let's face it: you always try to put your best foot forward when interacting with customers.

Your manager. Among the biggest complaints that project managers voice about their own manager is this: "My boss doesn't really know what I do or how I get things done." This is a fair criticism, as many managers don't get much of a glimpse into the daily lives of the project managers in their group. Curiously, they're not a good source of feedback either.

Once again, the point is this: the closer you get to the soft end of the competency continuum (Figure 3-1), the more you'll need to rely on yourself for self-improvement. For example: Take a moment to reflect on how you just interacted with that team member when you offered constructive feedback; consider whether you have personal biases that affect your competence; think about how jumping to conclusions about people impacts your ability to lead objectively.

One exception to the self-reliance concept: if you are fortunate enough to work with someone (1) whom you trust implicitly; (2) whose opinion you value; (3) from whom you can expect honest feedback; and (4) who is in a position to observe your on-the-job behavior, I strongly suggest you enlist his or her support in your quest for self-understanding.

Communication Skills and the Project Manager

This topic—and this skill—is so important, it deserves its own section. The ability to communicate effectively is widely viewed as crucial to success as a project manager. Consider the common observation that project managers spend at least 80 percent of their time communicating.

There are many communication approaches and many media to choose from. No matter what approach or media you choose, communicating effectively requires significant skill.

What Are Communication Skills?

Of the many ways to structure and list the skills required to be an effective communicator, it's most useful to think in terms of functional competencies or *communication abilities*. The most successful project managers I've known have had ability to:

- Express themselves effectively in conversations with management and customers
- Express themselves effectively in conversations with peers and team members
- Express themselves effectively in conversations with subordinates and support personnel
- Speak naturally before large groups
- Prepare and deliver formal presentations
- Speak off-the-cuff effectively
- Negotiate
- Write clear and concise notes and memos
- Write technical reports and other technical material
- Listen effectively
- Know when to talk and when to listen
- Provide constructive feedback
- Foster open communication
- Correct others tactfully
- Gauge whether a receiver understands a message
- Use vocabulary and terminology appropriate to the audience
- Interpret nonverbal communication
- Project poise and self-confidence

As you can see from the length of this list, communicating effectively requires a lot of skills. There are many books, articles, and training programs on communicating effectively, but one of the most important ways to improve your skills is to get into the habit of continuously monitoring and critiquing your communication style, asking yourself key questions, such as:

In interactive conversations:

- Do I speak clearly and at the right speed?
- Do I enunciate?
- Do I project my voice appropriately (not too loud or too soft)?
- Do I offer others sufficient opportunity to respond?

In oral presentations:

- Do I speak with confidence?
- Do I have any distracting mannerisms?
- Do I offer sufficient opportunity for reactions or questions?
- Do I use media appropriately?

In written correspondence:

- Is my choice of words clear and unambiguous?
- Does the message flow in a way that others can easily follow my train of thought?
- Do I avoid slang and colloquialisms?
- Do I use correct grammar?

Developing effective communication skills takes time, practice, and feedback. If possible, find an associate who can provide feedback on your skills and style. Because communication is such a difficult challenge, you should never stop working to improve your abilities and your approaches.

Basic Approaches to Communication

Your basic approach to communication affects the way your message is received and interpreted. For example, a phone conversation, a note, and a personal visit are all valid approaches to transmit *message content*. The choice to not communicate in person can alter the *interpretation* of your message. So before considering what medium (or method) to use, consider what is the best approach. Here are some choices.

Face-to-face or remote? Delivering a message in person often suggests a greater urgency to your message or a higher level of concern or consideration for the recipient. It is helpful if you expect an immediate dialogue to ensue. Face-to-face communication also affords you the opportunity to

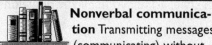 **Nonverbal communication** Transmitting messages (communicating) without using words. Nonverbal communication occurs through body position and movement, posture, facial expressions, clothing, behaviors, and in other ways. Nonverbal messages have the potential to replace, emphasize, or contradict verbal messages.

observe body language and other nonverbal communication.

Written or oral? Either approach has its advantages and disadvantages, and the preferred approach depends on your needs. Preparing a written message gives you the chance to rework the message until you feel it's right; however, written messages are subject to misinterpretation because tone, inflection, and feeling are difficult to convey. Verbal communication allows for more immediate back-and-forth communication; with that immediacy, however, comes the risk of saying the wrong things or saying things wrong.

Formal or informal? Your level of formality sends a signal. Formal communications may suggest a lack of familiarity, comfort, or friendliness with the other party. If you move from formal toward informal, you suggest that you feel (or would like to feel) that your relationship with the recipient is "warming." Formal communication also sends a signal that the content of the message is official—that you wish the dealings in question to be open, aboveboard, and not subject to manipulation. Most contractual dealings, for example, are formal, even if the parties know each other well.

Advanced preparation or impromptu? This issue is most relevant to face-to-face communication. If a situation requires thoughtful input, it may be best to make arrangements in advance, so both parties are aware of the subject and the timing of the communication. A person who is taken by surprise may provide an inappropriate or low-quality response. Setting up a communication session in advance takes time. Impromptu communications may provide a more candid response or offer the opportunity to observe a reaction.

In a group setting or one-on-one? Delivering messages to groups has two advantages: it's efficient and it ensures that everyone hears exactly the same message delivered in exactly the same way. An obvious exception to a group meeting occurs when the message is sensitive, such as situations where some members are personally affected or when proprietary information cannot be shared with everyone.

What Is the Best Communication Medium?

Once you've decided which approach will work best in a given situation, it's time to consider the optimal medium—or method—of communication. The options are many. Let's look at some of these methods and related considerations.

E-mail. Some contend that e-mail is an overused (and sometimes inappropriately used) medium. It's certainly convenient for most people. And while e-mails can reach widely dispersed and distantly located recipients quickly, there's no guarantee that the recipient will read the message right away. E-mails automatically provide a permanent record for the sender and receiver (which may be good or bad). Also, as with any written message, e-mails are subject to misinterpretation.

The ease with which e-mail notes can be forwarded to other parties should prompt you to be careful about what you put in the message and how you express yourself. All in all, e-mail is a convenient and effective method of communicating, if used properly.

> **MAKE SURE THE RIGHT PEOPLE CC YOUR E-MAIL NOTE**
>
> **TRICKS OF THE TRADE**
>
> Thanking someone for a job well done via e-mail can seem impersonal. However, making sure that the right people are included on your "cc" list can change all that. Copying a team member's supervisor on a note of congratulations or thanks is a powerful, effective, and easy way to provide recognition and positive visibility.

Telephone. Calling people on the phone can be an immediate (if they answer!), interactive way to communicate without creating a permanent, written record. Phone conversations allow you to hear voice inflections, although obviously you cannot view body language and other nonverbal communication. Although an upbeat phone call is considered "warmer" than a written note, it doesn't have the same effect as a personal visit or other face-to-face interaction. (The same holds true for unpleasant interactions.) Unanticipated phone calls are subject to the same shortcomings or advantages of impromptu communications.

Voice mail. When people don't answer their phone, you can often rely on voice mail. This may create issues for you, though, if you're not careful. When you place a call, you're often expecting a dialogue. If you have to use voice mail, you must immediately convert your message to a monologue, which doesn't always come out sounding as you'd like it. The message can become awkward or confusing to the recipient. And, as with e-mail, there's no guarantee that the message will be received in a timely manner.

Text messaging. Text messages are useful when the other party is unable to answer a phone call. However, there is no assurance that the message will be received, unless you request an acknowledgment. Since text messages are written, they suffer from many of the same issues encountered with e-mails.

PREPARE FOR YOUR RECORDING SESSION During your career, you've left some strange and curious voice messages for people. Why? Because you expect to reach the person you're calling—and are unprepared to get voice mail. The result can sometimes be a confusing "dialogue" with someone who isn't there, which can lead to misunderstandings. Before you phone someone, think about what you intend to say and how you can say it if you get sent to voice mail.

Handwritten notes. Probably the most informal of all communication methods, short notes written by hand are an excellent way to provide positive recognition. Although they usually take little effort, they convey "the personal touch" much more than verbal approaches or formal memos or informal e-mails. Among the drawbacks of these types of notes is that it generally requires people are working in the same place.

Printed and mailed memos and letters. With the advent of e-mail, memos and letters are now usually reserved for more formal or official communication. They're slow and one-sided, but good when formal signatures are required and a permanent record is desired. Hence, printed, mailed memos and letters are still used frequently in contractual situations.

Informal visits. A visit is ordinarily an informal and personal way to maintain communication with an individual. Although you may not be carrying a specific message, an informal visit often leads to a more valuable or productive communication session than you might get from a formal one-on-one or a group meeting. Informal visits are appropriate when confidential, personal, or sensitive subjects need to be covered.

Formal presentations. Formal presentations are often used in situations where the distribution of information may be enhanced by an explanation or the information is too complex for written documentation. Formal presentations are often done in a group setting, thus ensuring that everyone "hears the same message." Formal presentations allow for impressive graphical information displays, but often require a lot of preparation. Presentations are effective when you're trying to promote understanding, enlist support, or expedite a decision (e.g., management approval to proceed). However, formal presentations can be challenging or risky, as you rarely have control over the entire session.

Remote updating through project management software. This communication method is unique to project management. One of the newer features that some project management software companies are promoting is the ability for team members to provide project status to the project manager without a need to meet face-to-face. Although this communication method may be a boon for geographically dispersed teams, the software manufacturers fail to make that distinction. This leaves some project managers believing that it's better to get electronic updates from team members just down the hall than to meet with them regularly. This can be dangerous, though, as you forgo the opportunity to look team members in the eye and ask them how they're coming along on their activity—then observe their reaction.

General Guidelines for Communicating Effectively

Choosing the right approach and the best medium are critical communication decisions. But how do you actually go about the process of communicating? This may seem like overkill to some, but not taking the time to plan and failing to follow some basic guidelines can lead to disastrous results. Whenever you're communicating with others—face-to-face, in writing, by phone, or through memos—keep in mind these guidelines for effective communication:

Consider the function of the communication. Think about the purpose of your communication. For example, are you trying to provide information, offer an opinion, gain support, or drive a decision? This will affect how you structure the communication and what approach is best.

Get to the point. I've been subjected to countless phone calls and memos that took far too long to get to the point of the communication. Don't do that to others. Strive to be concise.

Apply what you learned in school. Pay attention to spelling, grammar, sentence structure, and composition when communicating—particularly in business writing.

Avoid distractions. Consider everything that may distract the recipient from getting the full impact of the communication and strive to reduce or eliminate anything that could cause confusion. Choose the right timing and physical setting. And be sure that your personal conduct isn't distracting.

Consider long-term effects. We often think of communication as being immediate and short lived. However, that's not always the case. What if your e-mail gets forwarded to the wrong person? What if you fail to include someone in a critical communication? Such matters may have long-term implications. Think about this when you're planning your communication.

Follow up. It's usually a good idea to follow up on your communications. Did the person receive the message? Did he or she understand it? Does he or she have any questions?

Conducting High-Quality Meetings

The subject of meetings requires special attention, as they are an important form of communication.

To most project managers, meetings are an important avenue for gathering and dispersing all kinds of information. Project team meetings are a common way to conduct project business. In addition to regularly scheduled team meetings, you'll find that there are many other times when you may need to call your group together. Unfortunately, many people view meetings unfavorably, so it can be a struggle to get people to attend, in part because they feel there are too many meetings and most are poorly run. If you develop a reputation for running effective, no-nonsense meetings, you increase your chances of consistently getting good attendance and valuable participation by attendees. Understanding when to call a meeting and learning how to run one are key skills that don't get sufficient attention in many organizations. Here are some tips about calling and conducting meetings—core team meetings as well as general meetings.

Determine whether a meeting is even required. You can avoid being viewed as "meeting happy" if you follow these basic guidelines:

- Don't call a meeting if a series of phone calls will serve the purpose.
- Don't call a meeting to decide something that you can or should decide yourself.
- Don't call regular team meetings any more frequently than necessary.
- Don't call a meeting if you're reasonably certain there's nothing new to discuss.
- Don't prolong a meeting if the group is through conducting the business at hand.

Be clear on the purpose of the meeting. Being clear on the meeting's objective will sharpen its focus and improve efficiency. Here are the basic meeting types and their purpose:

- Progress—assess status and accomplishments and to set more goals
- Decision—develop and agree on a decision
- Agreement—present a case on a decision and seek collective acceptance
- Information—communicate information or decisions that have been made
- Opinion—collect viewpoints and perspectives from participants
- Instruction—provide direction, enhance knowledge, or teach a skill
- Review—analyze some aspect of the project, such as design

Conduct all meetings in an organized and systematic way. Consider the following guidelines for conducting effective and efficient meetings:

Prepare for the meeting.

- Determine the objective or purpose.
- Prepare introductory comments.
- Prepare an outline of topics to present or discuss.
- Determine appropriate meeting duration.

- Invite the right individuals (the minimum required to accomplish objective).
- Tell participants how they need to prepare for the meeting.
- Notify participants in time to prepare; distribute the necessary materials.

Personally and visibly kick off the meeting.

- State the meeting's purpose.
- Review the background, if necessary.
- Announce the specific topics or problems to be discussed.
- Make sure everyone fully understands the topics or problems.

Ensure attention and participation.

- Encourage participation; allow everyone to contribute.
- Control discussion; drive out hostility; prevent monopolization by one person.
- Keep the discussion relevant to the meeting purpose!
- Keep things moving forward!
- Ensure that participants understand what's going on.

Close the meeting.

- Stick to the allotted time!
- Summarize by emphasizing what's been accomplished.
- Drive to development of an action plan if future work is needed.
- Clearly indicate what follow-up action is required; obtain commitment as needed.

Perform necessary follow-up.

- Prepare and distribute a record of conclusions or recommendations.
- Don't tell everything that happened in the meeting; be concise.

If you follow these suggestions, people will be more likely to attend your meetings. If people begin skipping meetings—particularly team meetings—information flow and general team communication will be hampered and you'll have to spend more time gathering information and attempting to correct behaviors.

Now that you completely understand everything there is to know about projects, project management, and the role of the project manager, you're ready to move on to defining the project.

Manager's Checklist for Chapter 3

☑ As a project manager, you have responsibilities in four broad areas: your project, your organization, your team, and yourself.

☑ One of your unspoken roles is to educate others in what project management is and how it works. Doing this benefits you in the long run—as you improve your understanding of project management, the smoother your life as a project manager is likely to be.

☑ The skill requirements of project managers are diverse and include process skills (project management tools and techniques), interpersonal and behavioral skills (getting along with and leading people), technology management skills (familiarity with technologies used in the project), and desired personal traits (your attitudes, values, and personal conduct). To be successful, you need to become proficient in each of these areas.

☑ Communication skills are of paramount importance to project managers. When you communicate, consider the optimum approach, medium, and process.

☑ You will probably have to perform a number of "unofficial" job duties in your role as project manager. Included on the list may be babysitter, salesperson, teacher, and politician. How often you need to perform these roles will depend on whom you work with and your organizational culture.

☑ Although you are surrounded by potential sources of feedback (e.g., team members, customers, and peers), you can't count on them for honest, accurate feedback on your performance. You must accept responsibility for your self-improvement. Develop the ability to be introspective. Periodically examine your performance and look for opportunities for improvement.

How Companies Identify and Select the "Right" Projects

I n most companies, the process of identifying and selecting projects is not ordinarily viewed as falling within the domain of project managers—or within the domain of traditional project management practices, like those we cover in this book. However, it's important to address this subject, as the methods that a company uses to identify and select projects—and the resulting impact this has on the quality of the projects selected—have a significant effect on the practicing project manager. Let's see how these concepts apply to Brad's situation.

After some brief soul-searching, Brad has decided that he's mentally prepared to take on his new role as project manager. He believes he understands what's involved and is eager to get to work. So is Gina, who has just called him into her office for a formal briefing. As she hands him a folder, Gina says, "Brad, here is the documentation I have for Project Apex. It was developed through a joint effort of our Marketing department and the Operations folks. I'd like you to get going on this project right away. OK?"

As Brad accepts the folder, Gina remarks, "Good luck, Brad. Oh, by the way, if you should have any questions or need anything at any time during the project, please know that my door is always open."

"Thank you, Gina," Brad answers with a confidence he's not sure he feels, "I'm sure I'll do a great job on Project Apex."

Brad heads back to his office, where he immediately leafs through the surprisingly thick project folder. Embedded in the documentation he has received is the stated customer need for Project Apex: "Install an additional production line in the manufacturing department and revamp the existing product distribution procedures." There is a section called Project Targets that states when the project will be completed and how much it will cost. There are also several design documents, charts that outline performance capabilities for the new line, and functional requirements for the new distribution procedures.

As Brad continues to review the project documents, he is feeling more and more troubled. "Something's missing," Brad thinks to himself. "I don't understand. I can see that they want me to put in a new production line and revise the product distribution system. That seems clear enough. But *why* are we doing this project? Is this even a worthwhile venture? Is this initiative as important as other projects we have going on now? Also, I don't see any schedule or detailed estimates, so how could they possibly tell when Project Apex will be completed and how much it will cost?"

Where Projects Should Come From

Brad has simply been handed a project—along with some prescribed cost and schedule targets—and told to "go forth and execute." It is not readily apparent to Brad whether his company conducted the appropriate preproject activities (those on the front end of the overall project life cycle shown in Chapter 2), and that's nagging at him.

Sadly, Brad's circumstance is not unique, and there's a good chance it could happen to you! While it may be uncomfortable for you as the project manager, it could actually be harmful for your company or organization. The organization could be wasting a considerable amount of time, money, and human resources—and missing critical business opportunities—by not using a sound process for identifying and selecting projects.

You (and your company) can be more certain that you are working on the "right" project if it satisfies these three simple, but necessary criteria:

1. It addresses an *established need.*
2. It is shown to be a *worthwhile financial investment.*

3. It is shown to rank among the *best opportunities*.

Closely aligned with these criteria are three critical and worthwhile processes:

1. Top-down planning (conducting a needs analysis)
2. Project financial analysis (conducting an ROI analysis)
3. Project prioritization (conducting a portfolio analysis)

Once again, although these activities are not the primary focus of this book, your understanding of project management—and your competence as a project manager—will be enhanced if you know more about these activities and how they may (or may not!) relate to your project. So let's examine them.

Critical Process #1: Identify Projects Through a Needs Analysis

A *good project* is a response to a problem, need, or opportunity. Whatever the original motivation may be, all projects will fall into one of two categories: strategic or operational.

Some projects come about as a result of annual planning meetings conducted by senior managers and executives. From these meetings, high-level organizational goals are established and growth opportunities are identified. This is called *top-down planning*, and it often leads to the formation of strategic initiatives—and eventually to the identification of strategic projects. The intent of *strategic projects* is to take a company or an organization to a new

> **BALANCING STRATEGIC PROJECTS AND OPERATIONAL PROJECTS**
>
>
> **SMART**
>
> **MANAGING**
>
> From a big-picture perspective, it's important that companies maintain a mix of strategic projects and operational projects. By doing this, they strike a healthy balance between "reaching for the stars" and "keeping the lights on."

and better place. Examples might include developing a new product or offering a new service to customers.

Operational projects are intended to optimize the way a company currently conducts its business. This can pertain to the company's core business (selling widgets, for example) or to business processes that support the core business (accounting procedures, for example). The objective of these kinds of projects is to increase the efficiency or effectiveness of current operations. Here, opportunities are typically driven by a quest for continuous improvement, the recognition of suboptimal performance, or the identification of a specific problem. Addressing these kinds of opportunities eventually leads to the identification of operational projects. The intent of operational projects is to improve the status quo. Examples might include increasing the throughput of an existing system or improving the efficiency of an existing process.

In general, the identification of all projects—whether strategic or operational—should result from a thorough needs analysis. A needs analysis is the best way to maximize the impact of project work on an organization. Figure 4-1 illustrates what a needs analysis might look like.

Framework for Identifying, Prioritizing, and Approving Project Investments

STRATEGIC OBJECTIVES	PERFORMANCE METRICS	KEY VALUE DRIVERS	PERFORMANCE GOALS
Reduce the **Cost** of Doing Business	■ Labor costs ■ Material costs ■ Waste costs ■ Cost of quality	■ Labor ■ Material ■ Waste Operating labor Maintenance labor Material consumption Internally induced waste Scrap costs Supplies usage	■ Reduce direct labor costs by 10% ■ Reduce waste by 15% ■ Reduce scrap costs by 25%
Meet **Demand** and Manage Supply Chain	■ Cycle time reduction ■ Inventory turns ■ Breakdown risks	■ Optimize asset productivity ■ Cycle time ■ Reduce inventory	■ Reduce cycle time by 3.5% ■ Reduce inventory turns to 0.4/week ■ Increase reliability by 7%
Meet or Exceed **Product Quality** Standards	■ Quality audit results ■ Alpha/Beta error rate ■ Trade reaction	■ Improve outgoing quality ■ Improve process control capability ■ Optimize on-time delivery	■ Reduce defect rate 10% ■ Reduce beta errors by 30% ■ Increase on-time ratio to 0.975

Figure 4-1. Example of a top-down needs analysis

Unfortunately, not all companies identify projects by conducting a rigorous needs analysis. In far too many companies, just about anything that "seems like a good idea" becomes a project. And while many of these project proposals may be well intended by apparently addressing a problem, the reality is that they begin their life as someone's *desired* action, not as a *logical response* to an established organizational need. Consequently, a substantial number of these projects may not result in the

---

ENCOURAGE THE USE OF A "TOP-DOWN" PROCESS   SMART

If you manage projects in an organization where it seems like every good idea turns into a project, you may be in jeopardy! In this environment, it is not unusual to later discover that some of these good ideas were not so good after all. And if you were the **MANAGING** project manager for one (or more) of them, your reputation may take a hit. So, if this sounds like the kind of approach your organization uses to identify project opportunities, why not suggest that it use a process based on conducting a thorough needs analysis—not on surfacing "good ideas."

---

achievement of long-lasting or meaningful change. As a project manager, you will find value in recognizing that you have been assigned to manage a *good idea* project (I explain why later).

Critical Process #2: Ensure a Solid Return on Investment

Among the biggest changes in the project management landscape over the past several years is a growing recognition that projects, while appearing to be simply large, well-planned actions, are actually unique financial investment opportunities. Companies have always been aware that they shell out a considerable sum of money to do projects. But there is now a growing sensitivity to one unavoidable reality: if a company pursues a project whose long-term financial return is not greater than the cash outlay required to execute it, it is—in the final analysis—losing money by doing that project!

This means that for any project—strategic or operational—one question must always be asked: From a financial perspective, should we be doing this project? This question can be answered by performing a project financial analysis. Projects that survive such an analysis are referred to as being financially justified. And while you may think that financially justifying projects would be a routine activity in all companies, it is not done with a great deal of frequency (if at all) in some.

Using Financial Criteria to Justify Projects

Though some companies do not routinely use financial criteria to justify projects, many do. In fact, many also use project financial analysis for project prioritization, which we discuss near the end of this chapter.

Conducting a project financial analysis (also referred to as a *cost/benefit analysis* or a *return on investment* (*ROI*) *study*) often includes some combination of these four metrics:

1. **Net present value (NPV).** Calculating a project's NPV answers the question: How much money will this project make (or save)? NPV is a calculation in dollars of the present value of all future cash flows expected from a project. It's roughly analogous to the concept of profit.

2. **Internal rate of return (IRR).** Calculating the IRR answers the question: How rapidly will the money be returned? It's a calculation of the percentage rate at which the project will return wealth. IRR is roughly analogous to the effective yield of a savings account.

3. **Payback period.** Calculating this metric (also known as *time to money* or *breakeven point*) answers the question: When will the original investment (the amount spent on the project) be recovered through benefits? The payback period is typically expressed in months or years.

4. **Cash hole.** Calculating the cash hole (also known as the *maximum exposure*) answers the question: What's the most we'll have invested at any given point in time? The cash hole is expressed in terms of dollars.

TRICKS OF THE TRADE

CHARACTERIZING METRICS

Here's how you might characterize a project's key financial metrics (Note: Some liberties taken!):

- Net present value (NPV): The profit that a project earns.
- Internal rate of return (IRR): How fast those profits are earned.
- Payback period: How soon the original investment is recovered.
- Cash hole: The depth of the financial hole created through project spending.

How a Project Financial Analysis Is Conducted

Each of the four financial metrics identified above can be determined by performing a project financial analysis. Although you may not be intimately involved in performing a complete financial analysis, as a savvy project manager you should understand how it's done and the terminology involved. The basic financial analysis process is not as difficult as many think. It consists of four basic steps.

Step 1. Identify the sources of cash flows (inflows and outflows). Executing a project causes money to flow in and out of a company. *Cash inflows* are the financial benefits that can be claimed as a result of executing your project: for example, an increase in revenue from sales, a reduction in production or operating costs, material savings, or waste reduction. *Cash outflows* are any expenditures or increases in ongoing operating costs due to the project or its downstream effects. The most obvious cash outflow is the cost of the project itself. But projects can also have a negative financial impact on a company long after the project is completed. These impacts must be included in the financial analysis of the project.

Step 2. Estimate the magnitude of specific cash flows. In some cases, it is fairly straightforward to estimate cash flows. In other cases, it's difficult. For example, consider how confident you would feel in placing a specific dollar value on these benefits:

- Increased output due to enhanced employee satisfaction
- Improvement in vendor delivery reliability
- Improvement in workforce safety
- Increase in user comfort or convenience
- Reduction in potential legal action against your organization

Solid, unbiased business judgment is often needed to estimate these types of cash flows. Using historical data or benchmarking data is also helpful.

Step 3. Chart the cash flows. After you've determined the sources of cash flows and estimated their magnitude, you are ready to construct a cash flow chart (an example appears in Figure 4-2). You should chart all cash outflows and inflows year by year throughout the useful life of the project.

KEY TERM

Useful life The period of time through which the assets created by a project are expected to be productive. This determines how far into the future a project financial analysis is conducted. This period can vary considerably—from 2–3 years for IT assets all the way up to decades in the case of durable assets such as buildings. Your accounting department ordinarily establishes the size of the window based on the type of assets your project produces.

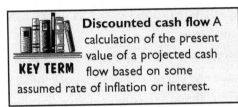

Once this is done, the net cash flow per year is calculated. The final step consists of making an allowance for the time value of money, using a technique called *discounted cash flow* (DCF) methodology.

Cash Flow Item	Year After Project Initiation										
	1	2	3	4	5	6	7	8	9	10
Cash Outflows										
R&D costs	−40	−20								
Capital costs		−80	−60							
Operating costs				−40	−40	−40	−40	−40	−40	−40
Cash Inflows										
Sales				+100	+100	+100	+100	+100	+100	+100
Maintenance				+15	+15	+15	+15	+15	+15	+15
Materials				+10	+10	+10	+10	+10	+10	+10
Waste				+5	+5	+5	+5	+5	+5	+5
Cash Flow/Year	−40	−100	−60	+90	+90	+90	+90	+90	+90	+90
Discounted Cash Flow/Year	−40	−91	−49	+67	+61	+56	+51	+46	+42	+38
Cumulative Discounted Cash Flow	−40	−131	−180	−113	−52	+4	+55	+101	+143	+181

Figure 4-2. Example of a project cash flow chart

Step 4. Calculate the net cash flow using an agreed-on discount rate. Because the value of a dollar in the future is less than the value of a dollar today, the value of any future cash flows in the cash flow chart must be *devalued*, or *discounted*. The rate used to discount future cash flows is based on how much it costs your company to acquire capital—typically done by borrowing money (loans to your company) or through equity financing (owner- or shareholder-supplied money). Your company's Accounting department ought to be able to tell you what the discount rate is for the type of project you're managing.

The cumulative total of all discounted cash flows through the useful life of your project is called the *net present value* (*NPV*). An NPV greater than zero indicates that your project is making money; that is, the project is expected to provide a financial return that exceeds the organization's investment. A positive NPV project would be considered financially justified.

The NPV of the project depicted in Figure 4-2 can be found in the lower right corner of the cash flow chart. This project's NPV is $181,000.

Calculating the internal rate of return (IRR) is trickier, and we do not go into detail on that here. (Applying a discount rate of 10 percent, the IRR of the project shown in Figure 4-2 would be about 20 percent.) This value represents the *effective annual yield* of a project. A project can only have a positive NPV if the IRR is greater than the cost to acquire capital (remember the discount rate?), and that is one of the main points of all these calculations!

The third financial metric, *payback period* (or *time to money*), occurs when the point in time at which the original investment (normally the project expenditure) has been recovered. At that point, the cumulative discounted cash flow is zero. In the project shown in Figure 4-2, this would occur near the end of Year 6.

Finally, the *cash hole* (or *maximum exposure*) occurs at the point where the cumulative net cash flow is the largest negative amount—how far the project is in the hole. In the example shown in Figure 4-2, the maximum exposure is expected to be $180,000; that occurs three years after project initiation.

[Note: For simplicity, some elements of this analysis have been omitted, such as the effects of depreciation and corporate income tax. My objective is to familiarize you with this process, not make you an expert. If your company routinely conducts project financial analysis, your Accounting group should be familiar with this process.]

Not all companies perform regular project financial analyses. In those companies, some organizational managers try to rationalize by claiming, "It's too much work," "We don't have precise numbers," "People can make up any numbers they want," and so forth. However, companies that don't establish the financial justification for the projects they pursue fail to recognize the risk they're taking. There's a real chance that a portion

PROJECT MANAGEMENT CAN HELP!
Many companies that routinely conduct project financial analyses do not invite their project management practitioners to participate. This represents an opportunity wasted. Formally justifying all projects—with the support of project management personnel and methodologies—ranks among the greatest opportunities for improving project management today!

If you are a project manager in a company that performs project financial justifications and you are not currently involved, demonstrate initiative by offering to help. You may bring much-needed discipline to the process, while gaining valuable insight into the motivating forces behind the project you are about to manage.

of the projects they authorize will lose money. These are the projects that are later deemed to have not met the desired business objectives.

Critical Process #3: Assess the Relative Value of Your Project

Whatever the method used to generate project proposals, it's common to end up with many more projects than the human resources (people) to do them. This suggests that organizations must ask two important questions: (1) How do we ensure we only pursue the best projects? and (2) How many projects can we tackle at a time?

The ability to answer both of these questions is rooted in a process known as *project prioritization*. Also called *ranking*, this process comprises three components:

1. A set of critical attributes (the factors)
2. An expression of the relative importance of the critical attributes (the weighting)
3. An evaluation scale (the scoring)

These components are typically incorporated into a *Weighted Factor Scoring Matrix* (also called a *Decision Matrix*). Figure 4-3 illustrates what a Weighted Factor Scoring Matrix might look like in an actual project ranking study.

The attributes and scoring should be established by considering the most important qualities of a certain type of project (product development,

Project Title	Net Present Value (0.50)	Market Life (0.15)	# of Users Affected (0.15)	Impact on Other Prods (0.10)	Technology Required? (0.10)	Total Score	Rank
	Project Attribute (Relative Weight)						
Project Alpha	4 / 2.00	3 / 0.45	2 / 0.30	4 / 0.40	4 / 0.40	3.55	1
Project Beta	2 / 1.00	5 / 0.75	3 / 0.45	5 / 0.50	4 / 0.40	3.10	3
Project Omega	2 / 1.00	3 / 0.45	4 / 0.60	3 / 0.30	4 / 0.40	2.75	4
Project Theta	3 / 1.50	3 / 0.45	4 / 0.60	5 / 0.50	2 / 0.20	3.25	2

Figure 4-3. Example of a Weighted Factor Scoring Matrix

infrastructure, or process improvement, for example). You may have noticed that I use the term *value* in the section heading. That's because a comprehensive ranking analysis typically incorporates a combination of financial and nonfinancial attributes. This is evident in the example shown in Figure 4-3.

However—again—many organizations do not routinely prioritize their projects. Why? Because they assume that every project that surfaces using the "good idea" approach will be executed. This leads to project overload, where every project—and every project manager—suffers, due to a general shortage of resources.

The three processes described above are not difficult to do. Like many other things in the world of project management, what's required is the will to do them, the discipline to do them correctly, and solid processes. More important, in the absence of these processes, there's an excellent chance that your company or organization cannot be certain it always identifies the right projects. And although you probably don't have the luxury of choosing which projects you're assigned to manage, you should do everything you can to avoid being assigned to projects that appear to have a suspicious origin.

Getting Off to a Good Start

If your company follows one or more of these processes, that's great! But even if it does, one final challenge remains: how much of the background information generated from the preproject analysis is shared with you?

Ideally, you want to understand the following attributes for any project you are assigned to lead:

- The motivation for doing the project
- The specific driving forces (the case for action)
- The financial drivers
- The strategic drivers
- The operational or functional drivers
- The few things considered to be the key value drivers
- The critical success factors

Project managers who understand these kinds of things are likely to do a better job managing their project on a day-to-day basis. They weren't just handed a solution and instructed to implement it—they truly understand why their project is being implemented.

 Project business case A document used by senior management to assess the **KEY TERM** advisability of a proposed project, to compare a number of projects competing for limited funds, or to assess the options around alternative solutions to a business need. The document incorporates a variety of compelling arguments and analytics that collectively describe why a project is worthy of management approval.

If the items listed above are not part of your initial project briefing, seek to understand them by asking questions. If your organization engages in the practice of writing business cases, many of the listed items should appear in that document. If the business case (or similar documentation) is not given to you at the project outset, ask questions. Find out as much as you can about the project for which you have assumed responsibility.

Manager's Checklist for Chapter 4

☑ While identifying and selecting projects is not typically viewed as part of their role, project managers should seek an understanding of how their company conducts these processes.

☑ All projects will fall into one of two categories: strategic or operational. Strategic projects take a company or an organization to a new and better place, while operational projects are aimed at improving and optimizing the current state.

☑ Projects are considered worthwhile when they address an established need; are determined to be a worthwhile financial investment; and represent the best opportunities.

☑ Using financial criteria enables a company to determine whether a project is a worthwhile opportunity; after all, when you boil it down, projects are really financial investments.

☑ Using a combination of financial and nonfinancial criteria is an excellent way to assess and rank the relative attractiveness of projects and (ultimately) to select the best opportunities. This approach allows for consideration of projects' characteristics that may be difficult to quantify in purely economic terms. A Weighted Factor Scoring Matrix is an excellent tool to conduct this type of analysis.

☑ Utilizing project management personnel and methodologies to conduct project financial analyses ranks high among the greatest opportunities for improving the overall management of projects today.

☑ Preparing a project business case document is an excellent way to consolidate and communicate the information, compelling arguments, and analytics that describe why a project is worthy of management approval; this document can also serve as an ongoing repository for project information as the project proceeds through its life cycle.

Planning and Estimating: The Foundation of Project Management

I t's often been said that project management consists of two major phases—doing the right project and doing the project right. Ensuring that your project is based on a real need and that it's justified from a business standpoint are two important aspects of doing the right project (as discussed in Chapter 4). Project planning, on the other hand, is all about doing the project right.

Project planning gets more attention than any other project management technique—and justifiably so. It's hard to imagine how a project could be successful without good planning.

In addition to being important, project planning is also an enormous subject and comprises two major aspects. The first is strategic in nature and consists of understanding the principles and philosophies of planning. The second component of project planning is tactical. It comprises the tools and techniques of planning, which are ordinarily used in conjunction with estimating methods. Estimating is a more challenging competency than many are aware.

Brad will soon realize that, once he formally accepts responsibility for managing Project Apex, he will transition from doing the right project to doing the project right, and will need to apply good planning practices immediately. During the time Brad will be defining his project (discussed in Chapter 6), he will be engaged in *preliminary*, or *high-level*, planning.

And as he prepares for execution by developing an Integrated Project Plan (discussed in Chapter 9), Brad will be engaged in *detailed* planning. The planning principles and philosophies outlined in this chapter are applicable to both types of planning. Let's take a look at some of the principles and philosophies of planning and estimating that Brad needs to know to be successful in managing Project Apex.

An Introduction to Project Planning

As much as we talk about project planning, it's difficult to characterize in a few words or graphics. Why? Well, for one thing, "the plan" can assume many shapes, sizes, and forms. And while many people equate "the plan" with the schedule, there's much more to a project plan than a schedule.

Creating an accurate, credible project plan requires a significant amount of effort and the input of many people. Attempting to create a project plan single-handedly has caused the downfall of more than one project manager. In essence, the project plan is a map that guides you and your team from beginning to end.

One reason that planning is so difficult to describe definitively is because project plans are always evolving. From the moment Brad transitions from asking, "What are we trying to accomplish?" (identifying the real need) to asking, "How are we going to accomplish it?" (defining the project initiative), he has started the planning process. Although he may not appreciate it right now, Brad will continue that process until the final days of Project Apex.

Organizations vary considerably in their approach to project planning. The specific procedures your organization prescribes reflect its philosophy toward project planning. If your organizational culture is action oriented (or simply does not believe in the value of planning), it's likely that your formalized planning procedures are minimal. In this environment, projects may be hastily initiated and planned, without properly considering alternative solutions or project risk and uncertainty.

Conversely, if your organization displays a bias toward certainty and control, that's probably reflected in the use of rigorous planning procedures.

About the Planning Process

Project plans evolve gradually. They are continuously modified and refined in terms of content, structure, and level of detail. The project plan must keep pace as the project definition becomes more refined, work is broken into ever-increasing levels of detail, assumptions are verified or refuted, and results are achieved.

Although many project planning methodologies exist, Figure 5-1 points out a common theme: project plans are often developed iteratively—at different times, at different levels of detail, and for different purposes. Major iterations are often tied to key decision points and result in the creation of different versions of the plan at different levels of detail and precision.

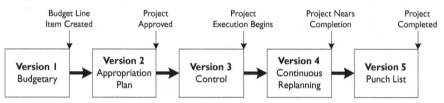

Figure 5-1. The evolution of a project plan

As Figure 5-1 shows, Version 1 of the project plan is developed before the project (as most people know it) has even been defined. This iteration is closely tied to the issues described in Chapter 4. In Version 1, there isn't much of a plan beyond the organization's intention to address a problem, need, or opportunity. Estimates of cost and schedule are just targets, or desired limits of time and money. It's done primarily for the purpose of allocating funds to an effort that will be listed in an organization's annual operating budget.

Version 2 of the project plan is created when the organization is prepared to initiate a project listed in its operating budget. Sufficient planning must be done so that it can be formally decided whether the project is an investment worth funding. The techniques and approaches used here are covered in Chapter 6.

If the project proposal is approved, Version 3 should emerge. It is a detailed plan that the project team will use as a guide for project implementation and that you will use continuously to evaluate progress and

CAUTION

PLANNING IS NOT A ONE-TIME EVENT!
It's inevitable that conditions will change during your project. Someone may be pulled off your team, resources may become unavailable when you need them, the business climate may shift, material shortages could occur, and so forth. As conditions change, your original plan must be modified to reflect those changes. The project plan is a living document, and you should expect to plan (actually, replan) throughout the project's life.

maintain control. The planning tools and methods used to create this version are covered in Chapter 9.

I like to refer to the next stage in the evolution of the project plan as *continuous replanning*. As the team implements the project, changes to the original project plan are a natural by-product. Based on progress and new information, your predictions of the project's outcome change, prompting you to make ongoing course adjustments. These continual changes should be reflected through slight plan modifications.

The last version of the plan, Version 5, is not mentioned in many project management books, but it can be vital to the success of a project. It occurs near the project's end, when it becomes apparent that a specific set of tasks (sometimes referred to as a *punch list*) must be done for the project to be considered complete. When you reach this stage, you may find it useful to create a brand-new plan to complete the remaining work. Creating a Version 5 allows for a highly focused and efficient effort and avoids being associated with the legendary "project that never ends." The approach used to generate this version of the plan is described in Chapter 12.

Beware! Common Planning Failures

Before diving into the details of how to create project plans, it's worthwhile to look at common mistakes that some project managers make in their planning approach.

Failure to do any planning. As you'll soon see, many factors influence the degree to which you should plan your project. Sometimes, a relatively small amount of planning effort will suffice. However, some project managers feel (or are pressured into feeling) that planning is not worth doing. Some action-oriented project managers—particularly new ones—feel that time spent on planning is lost. There's an interesting irony. When project managers don't plan, they spend a great deal of time fighting fires, so they're always going full speed. Since they're going at full speed, they rationalize their negligence in planning because they're too busy and don't have the time! Don't let this be you.

Failure to plan in sufficient detail. Sometimes project managers attempt to plan, but don't do it in enough detail. It's a question of how they size and compose elements of work—specifically the ones that they then put on their schedule and attempt to watch closely. It's important to be accurate and detailed when doing this. Failing to plan and schedule project work in sufficient detail results in problems down the line. You can avoid many problems by asking these questions:

- Will all involved participants readily understand what their tasks entail?

  You must describe and define the work elements in enough detail so that no one is confused. I've seen many cases where poor definition has resulted in considerable rework, as people misunderstood what was expected. For example, let's assume Brad's project contains a work element called "Analyze existing production lines." With no further explanation, Brad might believe he knows what this element entails. Think about it: would you be able to make an intelligent guess as to exactly what's included in this element? It's simply not defined in enough detail to avoid misinterpretation. One of the biggest factors causing confusion here is that this element is too big; it should be broken into subelements.

- Can you generate a reasonably accurate estimate of the duration and cost for this task?

  Work must be defined in a way so that someone can estimate its duration and cost with a high degree of confidence. This is consistent with a reality of project management: lack of detail in definition translates into higher levels of uncertainty—and therefore, risk. The less time and effort you put into defining your project, the greater the uncertainty in your estimate.

- Will you be able to effectively monitor progress on this task?

If you are to have any reasonable expectation of keeping your project on schedule, you must be able to gauge progress on tasks. The most convenient way to gauge progress is by observing the completion of small work elements (subelements) routinely—typically at project team meetings. Therefore, work elements need to be broken into enough detail that you can readily verify their completion.

SMART

MANAGING

SIZE THEM RIGHT!

There are two rules of thumb regarding how far to break down the work on a project so you can determine what work elements you'll put on your schedule and track. Both of these rules are reasonable and valid.

One popular rule of thumb suggests that you should size schedule items at around 40–80 labor hours.

The second guideline—and the one I recommend—suggests that you size schedule items proportional to the project—at around 4 percent of overall project duration. This sounds complicated (and mathematically messy), but it's not. For example, if a project will take six months, individual activities in the schedule should be about one week in duration. For a one-year project, the average activity duration would be around two weeks. And on an 18-month project, three weeks is a reasonable activity duration.

Failure to know when to stop planning. This is just as much a problem as not planning in enough detail. Some people believe that the further they break down the work, the more control they'll achieve. Not true.

For example, let's say that you're managing a 14-month project and you conduct team status meetings every two weeks. If you plan in such detail that your work elements are only a few days long, several of them may (or may not!) be completed between team meetings. So, you wouldn't benefit from your greater planning detail unless you were checking progress every few days. You will probably depend on the team's status reports at regularly scheduled team meetings (every two weeks), in which case, much of your schedule detail doesn't matter.

In addition, if your work elements are sized too small, creating the schedule and keeping it up to date could become an administrative nightmare. The paperwork involved—and the complexity of the project schedule—will not endear you to your team, either!

Failure to involve task performers in planning. The principle here is sim-

> ### Synchronization Is the Key
> The frequency of your team meetings and the size of the tasks on your schedule should be proportionate. If your project team meetings occur every two weeks, the average duration of your scheduled tasks should be around two weeks. Using this approach provides a reasonable balance between your need to maintain control and the amount of effort required to create and maintain your schedule. The 4 percent rule of thumb provides a good guideline for scheduling project team meetings as well as for sizing project activities on your schedule.

ple: the people who will be working on your project should be heavily involved in planning their own work. There are at least two good reasons for this. First, those actually performing the tasks are probably more knowledgeable than you about what has to be done—after all, it's what they do. Second, involving them during the planning stage makes them more willing to participate and more committed to successfully completing their tasks; people often feel compelled to live up to their promises.

Failure to reflect risk and uncertainty in plans. Chapter 10 is dedicated to the subject of risk and uncertainty. Why? Because it's a very big deal. Many projects are judged as failures simply because risk and uncertainty were not properly addressed. Risk management techniques use statistics and other scientific methods that help you make reasonable predictions—even under conditions of high uncertainty. Yet many who plan projects do not properly assess, accommodate, or plan for the inherent risk in projects. This happens for at least three reasons:

1. **Project managers don't understand risk management.** Although risk management techniques have been available for a long time, many project managers don't know how to properly address risk, so they ignore it. If you're unfamiliar with these techniques, make the study of risk management an integral part of your self-development plans.

2. **Project managers are victims of the "rose-colored glasses syndrome."** When managers prepare project plans, they tend to plan to an "all-success scenario." They visualize everything going perfectly. The problem is that this paints an unrealistic picture of the project's outcome. And projects planned this way have only one direction to go—downhill.

3. **Project managers yield to pressure from stakeholders, clients, or the market.** Incorporating risk and uncertainty in estimates may offer the appearance of extending schedules or increasing costs. That's an unfortunate and inaccurate perception, one that puts project managers under tremendous pressure to ignore or underplay the effects of risk. I once worked with a project manager who'd taken great pains to properly assess and plan for risk on his project. Unfortunately, this extended the most likely completion date beyond the deadline that had been imposed. He presented his thorough and thoughtful analysis to management, reporting that he would be unable to complete the project in the allotted time with a high degree of confidence, given the assumptions. What was management's reaction? "Fine, then we'll get somebody who can!" This didn't make the risk go away.

Failure to keep the plan current. For some project managers, planning is a one-time event. They create a plan to make a presentation to management and/or to get their project approved, and then store the plan on their shelf for the duration. Project plans *must* be kept current. They must continuously reflect what's occurring on the project. Variations from the original plan are inevitable. If you don't take these variations into account, it's harder to maintain control, chaos is more likely, and you hurt your chances of bringing the project in on time and within budget.

So ... How Much Planning Is Enough?

As is true of many questions related to project management, the answer to this question is .... It depends. In this case, it depends on many factors. Among the most important are the following.

Organizational expectations. As mentioned above, organizations have different perspectives on the value of planning. This reflects directly on the time and effort teams are expected to put into planning. It's vital that you understand your organization's expectations relative to planning. If they're low, I urge you to exceed them—to improve your chances of success. Just do it without a lot of fanfare.

Project importance. This factor is associated more with organizational

CONSIDER FITNESS-FOR-USE WHEN PLANNING

SMART MANAGING

When you're planning a project, one of the questions you'll face is how rigorously you plan to apply your organization's prescribed project management process. When answering this question, consider the concept of fitness for use—a term often applied in quality management and business law. In project management, *fitness for use* means to do what makes sense.

For example, imagine that your organization's prescribed project process has 50 steps. The fitness-for-use principle means that you should consider all 50 steps, but you may also recognize that—for a variety of reasons—only 43 of the steps add value, given your specific project circumstances. This saves you from losing time and wasting effort mindlessly following procedures. Before skipping any steps, however, make sure the appropriate stakeholders are aware of what you're doing, know why you're doing it, and agree with your decision to eliminate some steps.

politics than technical or logistical criteria. If you're politically astute, you'll realize that there's likely to be more attention paid to the so-called hot project than to other, more mundane projects. This is not to suggest that you should neglect planning for less glamorous projects—you just may be wise to put more into the planning and control of the high-visibility ones.

Project complexity. This point has more to do with logistics than money. Projects deemed as "small" could require a significant amount of coordination among parties—which may include intricate timing or a large number of participating work groups. Small projects often require more effort and forethought in planning. Conversely, it's possible that some projects could involve a very large expenditure (due to an expensive purchased item), but have a small number of activities. These projects wouldn't require a great deal of planning effort or detail.

Project size. Large projects generally require more planning than small ones. However, beware of a classic project manager mistake—taking this principle too far and underestimating the amount of time to be devoted to planning a small project. Small projects are often worthy of some extra effort in planning—proportionately speaking. The reason: small projects have a smaller margin of error. For example, while it would take a major incident to throw a large project 25 percent off target, it wouldn't take much of a problem to do the same to a small project.

> **Rolling horizon planning** If faced with a large quantity of unknowns at the outset of your project, you probably should not try to generate a *detailed* plan for the entire project. This
> **KEY TERM** gives the impression that you know exactly how the project will unfold—even well into the future. If your management asks you to produce the entire project plan at the outset of the project, you should (of course!) comply—just make sure you warn them that the predicted completion date may change (this topic is discussed in Chapter 10). You can reinforce your warning by displaying a schedule that shows great detail in the near term—for the next month or two, perhaps. After that, the schedule will clearly display a lower level of precision. This is often accomplished by using fewer activities with much longer durations (called *summary activities*).
>
> This pattern—displaying near-term precision and long-term vagueness in your schedule—will repeat itself many times throughout the life of the project, as new information presents itself and decisions are made. This technique is called *rolling horizon planning* (or *rolling wave planning*), and it's a logical planning process, particularly for any project that relies on a discovery or breakthrough, such as R&D or new product development projects.

Level of uncertainty. When a project's level of uncertainty is high, detailed planning of the entire project at the outset may be inadvisable, as you may find yourself guessing at far too many things. In fact, it may be a waste of time, due to the amount of change that's likely. On projects where the level of uncertainty is high, in the end you'll probably do the same amount of planning, but spread out over the life of the project. In other words, expect to spend a good deal of time replanning as you encounter change. This is called *rolling horizon planning.*

Project management software selection. Your choice of project management software (if you use it) affects your planning time. Obviously, the more user friendly the software, the less time you'll have to invest in using it. However, be aware that project management software products differ significantly in cost, capability, and utility. We discuss software in Chapter 9.

An Introduction to Estimating

Estimating is a big component of project planning. To prepare an accurate, thorough project plan, you'll need to estimate many things: how long it will take to do the work, how much the work will cost, how much money the project will save or make, the magnitude of the risk and uncertainty involved, and many other aspects. With that in mind, it's worth taking some time to discuss the estimation process.

It's Just a Guess, for Pete's Sake!

The dictionary defines *estimate* as "to judge roughly or approximately the value, worth, size, extent, or nature of." As most experienced project managers will tell you, the operative words in Webster's definition are *roughly* and *approximately*. The nature of project work is such that—even with significant prior experience—the uncertainty inherent in projects doesn't allow for absolute precision in estimates. Yet many people do not understand this point. As you manage more projects, you'll find this to be an issue with some people: they'll expect more precision and certainty in your estimates than you are able to provide. Consider this an opportunity to help them learn, to help them understand that, despite your best efforts to provide good estimates, "It's just a guess, for Pete's sake!"

Estimating Approaches

An estimate is a guess. But is there anything you can do to make it the *best possible* guess? Here's the answer:

- Ask the person responsible for doing the work to prepare the estimate.
- Ask a subject matter expert—a person with considerable knowledge of or experience in that area—to prepare the estimate.
- See if relevant estimating standards exist.
- Use historical data (actual past results) and interpolate as appropriate.
- Use mock-ups, trial runs, tests, field studies, or other simulated experiences to increase your knowledge.

The best approach depends on factors such as the availability of historical data, the estimating skills of task performers or subject matter experts, and the amount of time available to prepare an estimate. You may want to try more than one approach, and then apply your own judgment to come up with the best estimate. Keep two things in mind as you do this, though: the purpose of an estimate is to *model reality*—to reflect what is believed to be the most likely outcome. Don't be afraid to apply your own judgment to the input you receive, as long as you have a rational reason to do so. Finally, be true to yourself; resist being "pushed" into an estimate. Remember, you will probably be the person who is going to have to explain why your project cost as much and took as much time as it did.

Levels of Estimating Precision and Ranged Estimating

An estimating reality is this: The precision of any estimate is directly proportional to the amount of knowledge you possess. For example, it doesn't make sense to predict the completion date of your project within a day or two at the outset of any project. In fact, it wouldn't make sense to offer any *precise* estimates or predictions about your project. Here are a few examples why that's true:

- You haven't yet acquired knowledge of certain specific items (the agreed-on feature set of a product, for example).
- Certain aspects that impact your project are unpredictable (for example, currency exchange rates on an international project).
- Your project is expected to encounter several *decision nodes* (test results that could drive your project in one of several different directions).

We discuss these issues in Chapter 10.

As far as their relationship to estimating, refer to Figure 5-2, which is a combination of several popular models. This chart shows the relationship between the level of project knowledge and *estimating precision—* also referred to as *estimate classes*. It could pertain to cost or schedule estimating.

Stage of Project or Project Activities	Amount of Project Definition	Common Names for Estimates	Expected Range of Precision (from *most likely* point estimate)	
			Low	High
• Strategic Planning • Budget Line Item Created	Virtually none	Budgetary	−20% to −50%	+30% to +100%
• Feasibility studies • Initial investigation	Limited to very limited	Feasibility or factored	−15% to −30%	+20% to +50%
• Detailed investigation • Project funding Proposal	Moderate	Appropriation	−10% to −20%	+10% to +30%
• Detailed analysis of WBS (and project outcome is reasonably predicted)	High to very high	Definitive	−5% to −15%	+5% to +20%

Figure 5-2. Classes of project estimates

Estimating Pitfalls

Estimating is challenging, as there are many things that can undermine the accuracy or validity of any estimate. Among the most common pitfalls are:

- **Poorly defined scope of work.** This occurs if the work is not broken down far enough or individual work elements are misinterpreted.
- **Omissions.** Something was forgotten.
- **Rampant optimism.** This is the rose-colored glasses syndrome, where the all-success scenario is used as the basis for the estimate.
- **Padding.** This occurs when the estimator (often the task performer) includes a factor of safety without your knowledge, a cushion that ensures that he or she will meet or beat the promise.
- **Failure to properly assess risk and uncertainty.** This occurs when the estimator is aware of elements of risk and uncertainty, but doesn't know how to correctly incorporate them into the estimate.
- **Time pressure.** If someone says, "Give me a ballpark figure by the end of the day" and "Don't worry, I won't hold you to it," beware! This almost always spells trouble and results in underestimating because something is omitted.
- **The task performer and the estimator are at different skill levels.** Most people provide an estimate as if they were going to be the person executing the work. If the actual task performer works at a different efficiency level, a gap between the estimate and reality results.
- **External pressure.** Project managers are sometimes given specific "targets" of cost, schedule, quality, or performance (and perhaps more than one). This influences the estimate. If you're asked to meet unrealistic targets, you may not be able to fight it, but you should communicate what you believe is reasonably achievable.
- **Failure to involve task performers.** This practice may result in an ironic situation: an estimate developed without involving a particular task performer could be accurate, but that person may not feel compelled to meet the estimate, as he or she is thinking, "That's your number, not mine."

TRICKS OF THE TRADE

ASK FOR MORE THAN JUST "THE NUMBER"

Whenever someone gives you an estimate, remember that estimates comprise two dimensions: the estimate value itself and the level of certainty with which the estimator provides that value. To optimize your understanding of any estimate, always ask the estimator for these four things:

1. **The point estimate.** This is the number that estimators will give you initially. This value represents the most likely outcome (in the mind of the estimator).
2. **A range of possible outcomes.** Due to the effects of risk and uncertainty, the actual outcome of any estimated value could fall somewhere within a range of values. The question is: How large is that range? The size of the range should reflect the estimator's specific knowledge of whatever he or she is estimating.
3. **The basis for the estimate.** This is a description of how the estimated value was calculated and the assumptions used to arrive at that figure. This information can also offer valuable insight when changes occur later.
4. **Factors that affect the estimate validity.** Some estimates are based on volatile factors. Others have limitations beyond which the validity of the estimate cannot be assured. For example, will your estimate be valid three months from now? Will it be valid if the work is subcontracted? Is it valid throughout the United States or only in the Northeast?

Contingency: Then and Now

Contingency is a concept—and practice—that has been around for a long time. *Contingency* is defined as an amount added to any baseline estimate as an allowance for uncertainty, risk, unknowns, and omissions. I like to describe the purpose behind the addition of a contingency this way: Imagine you are at the beginning of a project. You cannot possibly know how it will turn out—there's too much uncertainty and risk ahead. However, you've been asked to produce an estimate that represents your best attempt, most notably in terms of cost and schedule.

A powerful combination of your knowledge of the project, your sense of what you don't know, previous project experience, the documented experiences of other project managers, and some good old-fashioned personal judgment leads you to conclude that an estimating shortfall exists. In other words, there's a gap between what you can "see, feel, and touch," and where you know you'll end up at project completion. This gap is created by your inability to understand exactly how to synthesize all the unknowns and uncertainties. According to good project management practices, the gap should be filled by applying a contingency.

But the pressure to do things faster, cheaper, and more efficiently has grown intense—often unrealistically so. In this environment, a contingency is sometimes viewed as a target for "cutting out excesses," which is not a good idea. As discussed, using a contingency is a legitimate estimating practice. There is also a perception by some that a contingency is no more than a slush fund for mistakes, as the contingency is typically something tacked onto the bottom line. This is an improper assumption, which has created even more estimating challenges for project managers.

Help has arrived, however, and I strongly urge you to use it. There are software products that use statistics to help you painlessly calculate contingency to accommodate risk, uncertainty, and unknowns. Although there are some slight differences, most work the same way. You provide ranges of possible outcomes for individual work elements. Then the tool can simulate the execution of your project thousands of times. The outputs associate a range of project outcomes correlated to various levels of confidence (confidence in your ability to meet or beat that particular outcome). This approach is discussed in Chapter 10.

Manager's Checklist for Chapter 5

✓ The project plan is more than a schedule. It comprises many documents.

✓ Project planning is not a one-time event. You'll probably prepare several iterations of the project plan in increasing levels of detail as you move through the project.

✓ Expressing estimates in terms of ranges of outcomes, rather than precise numbers, helps others understand the uncertain nature of projects. The size of the range should be proportionate to the degree of uncertainty.

✓ If the length of the work elements on your schedule is about the same as your team meeting frequency, you'll optimize project control. It's reasonable to make both about 4 percent of the overall project length.

Defining and Launching Your Project

Brad has come a long way since that first wave of panic hit him when Gina made him a project manager. He can recall the strange sound of the term *my project* the first few times he said it out loud. But he has come to like the way it sounds. And why shouldn't he? He's learned a lot in a short time.

Brad has learned that project management is both a science and an art—partly mechanical, partly behavioral. He believes he knows what it takes to be a good project manager and what it takes to produce a successful project outcome. He's certain that being a project manager is something he wants to do.

He has just finished reviewing the business case for Project Apex with Gina.

"OK, Brad," remarks Gina, "There's no doubt Project Apex is a valuable project investment. It's time get going. Right now your mission is to properly define your project and get it off the ground as soon as possible." As he leaves Gina's office, she adds, "Don't forget, I'm here if you need me!"

Brad is happy to be getting support from Gina, but he's still unhappy about the way he was handed a project without being involved in the project approval process. He vows that when he manages his next project, he'll try to make sure he's involved earlier in the life cycle.

On returning to his office, Brad leans back in his chair as he finishes his sandwich. He reflects on the reasons for doing Project Apex—the answer to the question of why it's being done. He understands the problems, needs, and opportunities that support his project, and thinks about the best way to address them.

Suddenly he lurches forward in his chair.

He just realized that decision has also been taken out of his hands. In addition to being handed the project, he was handed the solution! Brad has already learned enough to realize that this is not an ideal situation. "Oh, great," he groans. "I've officially been a project manager for less than 20 minutes, and I'm already encountering a crisis!"

SMART

MANAGING

Push for Early Involvement

What Brad is experiencing at the outset of his involvement with Project Apex is a scenario that plays out in too many organizations—he's been assigned to manage the project *after* a considerable amount of up-front work has already been done. The reason for this is that many organizational managers believe that a project manager's only role is to lead the actual execution of the project work. The reality is that assigning a project manager early on adds considerable value to defining and quantifying needs, determining optimal solutions, gathering project requirements, preparing project proposals, writing project business cases, and a host of other activities done in the early stages of project initiation. It also enhances the project manager's understanding of why the project is being implemented, which leads to better decision making throughout the project. So if you can, urge your management to formally assign a project manager as early as possible.

A Common Challenge in Project Definition

Brad is definitely correct. This is not an ideal situation—not from the viewpoint of the project manager, that is. Project Apex has been defined without his involvement. He is now expected to implement a specific solution—install an additional production line in the manufacturing department and revamp the existing product distribution procedures—and he can't be certain that's the best solution.

Once again, Brad has fallen victim to a problem that's common in many organizations. Someone has decided on a project, packaged it, then "thrown it over the wall"—and Brad is the lucky recipient!

Brad is concerned. And he is reluctant to move forward with Project Apex not knowing whether a valid process was used to reach this point. By raising this issue, he's demonstrating that he is better at project management than he realizes.

The Phenomenon of Solution-Jumping

Brad's concern is well founded, as one of the most common threats to excellence in defining projects is a phenomenon called solution-jumping. *Solution-jumping* is a product of human nature. It begins when we spot a problem. Rather than following a disciplined, analytical approach, our natural tendency is to want to solve it right away—often with the first solution we think of. On the surface, this appears to resolve the problem swiftly and decisively. Unfortunately, it's counterproductive to good project management, as it does not follow a data-driven, systematic, time-tested process. And it may have happened to Project Apex.

Let's help Brad navigate the process of properly defining his project and getting it started correctly. This way, Brad (and you!) will know

> **Solution-jumping** The tendency to take action before adequately analyzing a problem, need, or opportunity. Human nature—and the perpetual desire to do things faster—drives many people to suggest an answer without thoroughly understanding the problem. While this behavior may seem to save time and make someone appear "decisive," it could result in a significant waste of time, money, and resources if the solution is later found to be ineffective. **KEY TERM**

what a good process looks like, and be well positioned to ask the right questions, should challenges arise.

At a minimum, the process for getting your project defined and launched should consist of these four steps:

1. *Thoroughly understand* the problem, need, or opportunity.
2. *Determine the optimum solution* to the problem, need, or opportunity.
3. *Further define* your optimum solution and *develop a preliminary project plan.*
4. *Formally launch* the project.

Now let's take a look at each step.

First, Thoroughly Understand the Problem, Need, or Opportunity

Problems, needs, and opportunities can arise anywhere inside or outside the organization. *Problems* are generally regarded as a negative situation—something that needs to be "fixed." *Opportunities* are viewed as the positive, upside alter ego of problems. *Needs* frequently result from the recognition of some kind of performance gap.

Sometimes, the motivating force behind a project is tied to your company's external environment and is based on strategic considerations, such as:

- Recognizing a demand for a new product or a rapidly growing market
- A desire (or need) to increase customer satisfaction
- Addressing a problem with the corporate image or reputation

In other cases, the motivation comes from within your company and is driven by an interest in improving organizational performance. For example:

- Recognizing a need to simplify a costly and inefficient procedure
- The prospect of strikes suggesting a need to improve management-employee relations
- Organizational units spreading across a wide geographic region not communicating effectively

Developing a thorough understanding of problems, needs, or opportunities is more challenging than you may think. Sometimes they're very complex—a tangle of considerations. Experience has taught me that there is often more to a problem than what's apparent at first glance.

Sometimes you may be told what the problem is, but it is an incorrect diagnosis—or what you've been told is actually a symptom of the problem, not the problem itself. Sometimes you may be confronted with both of these issues.

No matter what your situation may be, remember this: it's in everyone's best interest to devote adequate time to fully understand all aspects of a problem before trying to solve it. What seems obvious or readily apparent may be masking a broader or more fundamental issue. The

AMY'S NEED

Luis walked briskly over to Bill's cubicle. "Bill, I just got a call from Amy. She's got a problem and has asked us to help. I'd like you to meet with her and get the details. Figure out what she needs and get it taken care of—right away."

By the following afternoon, Bill was sitting in Amy's office, carefully reviewing the documents she'd prepared.

"Bill, what we need is the ability to screen all our product components before they enter the final assembly line," said Amy. "Now you're free to do this any way you'd like; just make sure that whatever you do complies with these guidelines." With that, Amy handed Bill some design documents and a list entitled Incoming Component Screening Requirements.

Bill was happy that Amy had given him free rein to determine the best way to address her need. He studied the requirements and formed a project team. He and his team designed and installed the hardware and software necessary to check all incoming components for compliance with the screening requirements. It was truly a thing of beauty. Bill was proud of the job he and his team had done.

Less than a week later, Luis called Bill into his office. "Bill, Amy just called me," he said. "They're still experiencing exactly the same problem as before—there are too many rejects coming off the end of their final assembly line. What happened?"

Suddenly Bill realized what happened. He had just learned of Amy's *true need* ... the hard way.

process of cutting through the complexity, confusion, and ambiguity is referred to as *identifying the true need*. The importance of this step cannot be overemphasized.

Identify the True Need

The term *true need* refers to the most basic issue to be addressed. It's the underlying problem, the root cause. It's vital that you—as the project manager—understand what the true need is.

Why? Because many will judge you as a project manager by your ability to solve the original problem. And you cannot be certain that you have solved the original problem without fully understanding the true need.

The problem is that when you're assigned to manage a project, you may not be presented with the true need. Terminology can become confused: what's described as a need may actually be the solution to a need.

In fact, this is exactly what happened to Brad on Project Apex. The

---

> **THE VALUE IN IDENTIFYING THE TRUE NEED**
>
> Identifying the project customer's true need easily ranks among the most important steps in the entire project management process, as it establishes the foundation for identifying an optimal solution. It is almost impossible to be certain you are doing anything of long-term consequence without having a thorough understanding (and quantification) of the underlying problem, need, or opportunity.

---

documentation he received in the briefing identified the "need" as installing an additional production line in the manufacturing department and revamping the existing product distribution procedures. There's a big problem, though. What Brad was given was actually a solution—not a problem. Though Brad has sensed this intuitively, Figure 6-1 lists some key indicators he can use to confirm his intuition.

A Project Requirement (a stated need)	A Project Solution (a proposed project)
Describes the desired *end state*	Describes the *means* to an end state
Specifies the goals and targets, but does not suggest tactics or methods for achieving them	*Specifies the tactics and methods* for achieving goals and targets
Leaves open the question of "how" to do something	*Closes the door* on the question of "how" to do something
The answer to "why are we doing it" will yield the *business justification*	The answer to "why we are doing it" will yield the *project requirements*

Figure 6-1. How to tell the difference between needs and solutions

Most books on project management deal only with the mechanics of managing projects and helping you manage the project you've been assigned. However, properly identifying and quantifying the true need are actually more important than planning and executing the project. It's often been said that it doesn't matter how well you manage your project if you aren't working on the right goal. Bill just found this out the hard way with Amy's need (see "For Example" sidebar).

One of the most reliable methods for uncovering the true need is to ask the right people one simple question: "Why?" You may have to ask this question a few times before you uncover the true need. And as you seek to uncover the true need, you can expect to encounter some resistance.

Asking questions—rather than digging in and getting the project going—may give some the impression that you're wasting time. The reality is that working on an improper or ineffective solution is likely to consume much more time and resources in the long run.

TREADING ON THIN ICE
As you seek to understand what the client's true need is by asking questions, some people may feel threatened or offended. It may appear as if you are second-guessing or questioning the judgment and decisions of those who were involved in the initiative prior to your involvement. As you dig for answers, make sure everyone understands that this is not your intent.

This is exactly what Brad is thinking as he decides to do a little investigating.

Bothered that he doesn't understand the underlying purpose of Project Apex, Brad returns to Gina's office. "Gina, can you tell me why they want us to put in this additional production line?"

Gina thinks for a moment. "No, I can't," she replies. "But Milt in Operations might be able to tell you."

"Thanks a lot, Gina," Brad says as he exits her office. Later that day, Brad sits down with Milt and asks him the same question. "Milt, can you tell me why you need an additional production line?"

Milt looks quizzical. "Why are you asking, Brad? I don't understand why you're asking."

"I'd just like to try to understand the project details better," Brad responds.

"OK," says Milt, reluctantly. "Well, we need another production line because we can't meet the growing demand with the four lines we have now." Then he adds, "When we put these lines in four years ago, we were anticipating an output of about 800 units per week, but we're only getting around 600. It wasn't really much of a problem until recently, when we realized we wouldn't be able to meet demand by the end of the year. That's why we need another line."

Brad feels as if he has moved one step closer to identifying the true need with his first "why." Then, in a bold move, he decides to try the magic question one more time. "Why do you think you are only getting 600 units per week, Milt?"

At this point, Milt has obviously had enough. "If you need any more information, go talk to Monica. She was the lead engineer on the install."

As Brad is leaving, Milt repeats, "Brad, we really need you to get going on this new line right away, OK?" Brad just nods and smiles.

Before setting up an appointment with Monica, Brad reflects on the situation. The "need" presented to him is to install a production line in Operations. But his talk with Milt revealed that the true need is that they would not be able to meet demand by the end of the year because they're not getting the anticipated output from their existing production lines. It doesn't take Brad long to figure out that if he can improve the efficiency of the production lines from 600 units per week to 800, his client may be able to avoid putting in a new production line. That would likely save a lot of time and money—and resources! Brad feels good about where this is going. He senses a real opportunity as he picks up the phone to call Monica.

Brad's experience is not uncommon in the process of identifying and understanding true needs. It represents an excellent example of solution-jumping, and it happens all the time in the real world. In Brad's case, the four existing lines can't meet demand, so someone decided that a fifth line was needed. In fact, this could have been a snap judgment. And while installing a fifth production line would enable his customer to meet demand, it may not be the best way to fulfill that need. To be a superior project manager, Brad should make certain he pursues the best possible solution.

To do this, he must define, describe, and quantify all the parameters that characterize the best solution. Brad has some work to do; he needs to develop a Project Requirements Document.

Prepare a Project Requirements Document

The true need often starts as one or two brief statements. Now it must be further developed to a greater level of detail. The best way to accomplish that is by developing one of the most basic and important project management documents of all—the *Project Requirements Document* (or *Client Requirements Document*). The length of the requirements document can vary from one to several pages.

The following items should be part of a comprehensive Requirements Document.

PROJECT REQUIREMENTS DOCUMENT ETIQUETTE
The key to a properly written Project Requirements Document is simple: it should never offer a solution; it should only describe a need. (Refer to Figure 6-1.)

- **General description of the problem, need, or opportunity.** A narrative that outlines (in several sentences) the problem to be solved, the deficiency that's been discovered, or the opportunity that could be exploited. It might also describe how the need was discovered.

- **Impact or effects of the problem.** A brief description of the difficulties, challenges, circumstances, or events encountered because of the problem, need, or opportunity.

- **Identification of who or what is affected by the problem.** May be stated in terms of individuals, departments, or organizations—or the company as a whole.

- **Impact of ignoring the problem or opportunity.** A prediction of any future consequence (normally an undesirable one) expected to result from not addressing the situation. This is also referred to as the *inaction risk*.

- **Desired outcome.** Characterizes the ideal future state—what the world would look like if the proposed solution is successful. It is ordinarily described in terms of objectives, goals, targets, critical success factors, and key results. Generally, it should not identify specific deliverables, as deliverables tend to be associated with solutions, not problems.

- **Value or benefit associated with achieving desired outcome.** What an organization gains by successfully addressing the problem, need, or opportunity. It should be subdivided into two categories: financial benefits and nonfinancial benefits. Nonfinancial benefits are sometimes called the *intangibles*, or *soft benefits*.

- **Strategic fit.** Intended to address the question: Is the pursuit or is the execution of this project going to be compatible with our current set of organizational strategies? This is particularly relevant for opportunities.

- **Interface integration and compatibility issues.** Describes how this project opportunity or the satisfaction of these objectives may relate to other aspects of the organization.
- **Uncertainties and unknowns.** Also known as *action risk*; identifies missing data, information, or facts. May limit the accuracy or validity of certain predictions related to the ability to achieve the stated business results or impacts. May be a trigger for activities such as pilot tests, prototypes, surveys, and other information-seeking methods.
- **Key assumptions.** Assumptions ordinarily take the place of missing information. They represent anticipated values or conditions that may or may not be known to be true or readily verifiable. Assumptions are directed primarily at the business need and the environment surrounding that need.
- **Constraints.** Anything that is a limitation to a successful solution. Could include time, funding, resources, technology, or processes.
- **Environmental considerations.** Potential impacts, effects, or dependencies that the solution may have beyond the project boundaries. Some categories of environmental considerations include business/financial, marketing, operations, users, and technology.
- **Background or supporting information.** The repository of all information or research that has led to this point. Examples could include historical data, results of supporting studies, tests or survey data, marketing situational analysis, benchmarking data, or prototype test results.

Conduct Reality Check #1: Stop or Go?

Although it is early in the life of the project, two important questions should be asked once the Project Requirements Document has been created:

1. Is this problem worth solving (verifies financial justification)?
2. Does a potential solution exist(verifies feasibility)?

If you do not address these issues now, you run the risk of wasting time and money on problems that should not or cannot be solved. And if you lack detailed information at this point, that's all right. All you're trying to do at this point is preclude a large expenditure of resources on problems that don't have a cost-effective or practical solution.

The first issue—*verifying financial justification*—may be a challenge, as not much is really known about the project solution. Nonetheless, it's wise to assess whether you can justify continuing the project. Financial justification is established by comparing benefits against costs.

The benefit component of such an analysis is often easy to estimate: it's the financial impact of satisfying the need. It's the value of solving a problem or exploiting an opportunity.

But sometimes estimating the cost of the solution is challenging because you lack insight into exactly how you will address the need. You may need to speculate on solutions and how much each would cost. Or you might work backward through the financial analysis. By doing this, you may be able to determine the maximum amount that should be spent on a solution to cost-justify it. If you can't identify a solution that falls within that cost parameter, you know there's no cost-effective solution to the problem and probably should abandon the effort. The critical point to be made here is that you haven't wasted a great deal of time, money, or resources before making that determination. These concepts were explored in Chapter 4.

The second issue—*verifying feasibility*—comes down to a basic question: Do you believe that a viable (or practical) solution exists? In other words, can this problem even be solved? There could be a considerable amount of subjectivity in this step, as you will rely heavily on the judgment of subject matter experts. In reality, though, the most you can realistically hope to determine at this point is that the possibility of a solution exists.

Second, Determine the Optimum Solution to the Problem, Need, or Opportunity

Reaching this step suggests you've successfully navigated past solution-jumping. You thoroughly understand the need and you have established that satisfying the need is both justifiable and feasible. You have described the characteristics of an excellent solution. You are now ready to determine the best way to satisfy that need. Although I'm using the word *you*, proper execution of this step really requires input from many individuals. If you're fortunate enough to be involved at this stage of the project's evolution (remember, Brad wasn't), you should be actively working toward building a team from this point on (we discuss how to do that in Chapter 7).

Bear in mind that solutions identified through an initial, knee-jerk response—though they might solve the problem—may not represent the most effective approaches. The key to excellence in executing this stage of project definition is to be certain you have determined the best solution and the best approach—not just one that will work. This requires the application of careful thought, proper analysis, relevant expertise, and appropriate evaluative criteria. This process begins by considering several possible solutions.

Identify Several Alternative Solutions

Identifying the optimal way to satisfy the project requirements begins by generating a list of potential solutions. This process is greatly enhanced in the following ways:

- Do it in a team environment.
- Include subject matter experts and stakeholders as appropriate.
- Use brainstorming techniques.
- Limit further development to only reasonable alternatives.

TOOLS

BRAINSTORMING

Brainstorming is a group-oriented technique that involves the spontaneous contribution of ideas from all members of a team or group. Here are some tips on how to get the most from your brainstorming session:

- Stress the quantity of ideas over quality of ideas at this point.
- Encourage every group member to contribute any and all ideas.
- Do not be concerned with reasonableness or feasibility until you are done brainstorming.
- Do not criticize, judge, or evaluate contributions until you are done.
- Aggressively encourage the practice of combining or modifying ideas already identified to form new ideas.

Select the Best Alternative

Obviously, you can't pursue every idea identified through a process like brainstorming. After soliciting all reasonable alternative solutions, the project team needs to pare the list to only those worthy of further development, investigation, and definition. You can reduce the list by comparing each alternative against predetermined criteria.

This is where the Project Requirements Document adds significant value. The optimum solution is the solution that does the best job of satisfying the criteria stated in the Project Requirements Document. You may also choose to incorporate additional criteria meaningful to your project circumstance, such as the likelihood of technical success, the anticipated impact on existing products, or the availability of key resources. Using valid criteria, conduct an initial screening of proposed alternatives to reduce the size of the list to a manageable number—perhaps 2 to 4 ideas.

At this point, the selection process becomes more rigorous, as you will investigate each alternative in depth. It's time to bring out the decision matrix again!

Design a Decision Matrix to Assess Alternatives

Do you remember the Weighted Factor Scoring Matrix—or decision matrix—from Chapter 4? It did an excellent job of assessing the relative attractiveness of a number of proposed projects. The same tool can be used here. This time, though, you'll assess alternatives instead of projects. Let's examine it again.

Figure 6-2 shows what a decision matrix might look like in an alternatives analysis. With this example, we identified five criteria that would be valuable in a comparison of alternative solutions. Note that two criteria are financial

> **WEIGHTED FACTOR SCORING MATRIX**
>
> The Weighted Factor Scoring Matrix (decision matrix) is a comparative method for selecting the preferred alternative based on certain predetermined criteria. Although it does not provide absolute verification of financial justification, it offers a sound method for selecting the best among several alternatives. The decision matrix works best when a combination of financial and nonfinancial criteria are used.
>
> **TOOLS**

(net present value and estimated cost) and three are nonfinancial (how well it satisfies our window of opportunity, how user friendly it is, and whether we have the existing resources to support its implementation). We then weight each attribute by assessing a relative importance (or weight) to it. To function properly, this set of numbers must add up to 1 (or 1.00).

Alternative ID	Alternative Criteria (Relative Weight)					Total Score	Rank
	Net Present Value (0.40)	Estimated Cost (0.10)	Window of Opportunity (0.20)	User Friendly? (0.20)	Existing Resources? (0.10)		
Alternative 1	2 / 0.80	2 / 0.20	4 / 0.80	4 / 0.80	3 / 0.30	**2.90**	2
Alternative 2	3 / 1.20	4 / 0.40	3 / 0.60	3 / 0.60	2 / 0.20	**3.00**	1
Alternative 3	2 / 0.80	2 / 0.20	4 / 0.80	3 / 0.60	4 / 0.40	**2.80**	3
Do Nothing (business as usual)	2 / 0.80	5 / 0.50	1 / 0.20	1 / 0.20	5 / 0.50	**2.20**	4

Figure 6-2. Using a decision matrix to identify the best alternative solution

You need to establish a scoring scale for your decision matrix. The example shown in Figure 6-2 displays a simple five-point rating scale. The design of scoring scales is different for each criteria. Be sure to clearly define each of the scoring scales—everyone must have a common understanding of what a particular score (1, 2, 3, 4, or 5) means exactly for each criteria. Once you've established the relative weighting and the scoring scales, it's a question of filling in the blanks. The score in each box describes how well a given alternative satisfies that particular criteria. In our example, Alternative 2 was determined to be the most attractive choice.

Using a Weighted Factor Scoring Matrix offers many advantages:

- It largely eliminates the arguments that would take place in an open and unstructured debate on what constitutes the best alternative.
- It virtually eliminates the likelihood that an alternative will be chosen by any single individual.
- It forces the use of a wide variety of the most meaningful decision criteria.
- It is easy to construct and interpret.
- It is a good vehicle for soliciting input from organizational managers, as they can play a valuable role in determining the appropriate criteria and their relative weights. In fact, involving management in constructing the matrix is likely to facilitate the formal project approval process.

There are also some disadvantages:

- The process relies heavily on subjectivity, leading to potential concerns over bias, halo effects, and favoritism.
- The result obtained is only a measure of relative attractiveness. There is no absolute verification that any of the alternatives is a justifiable investment from a business perspective.
- All attributes are assumed to be independent; there are no allowances made for interdependencies among factors.

TIPS ON EFFECTIVELY USING THE DECISION MATRIX

TRICKS OF THE TRADE

Use a combination of financial and nonfinancial criteria to ensure a comprehensive analysis of alternative solutions. Adjust weights to reflect how dominant you'd like each criteria to be. Always include one or two financial metrics as attributes. Financial criteria should ordinarily be weighted heavily. To save effort and simplify your analysis, only include alternatives that are financially justifiable in your decision matrix. Using more than six criteria is not recommended, as that begins to trivialize the impact of some criteria. If all alternatives yield exactly the same score for a particular criteria, that criteria is an ineffective differentiator; eliminate it and identify another.

Don't Forget the "Do-Nothing" Scenario

Here's an item from the "hot tip" file: any time you assess alternatives, always evaluate the advisability of taking no action on the problem, need, or opportunity. This is commonly referred to as the *do-nothing scenario*. Do not be fooled into thinking that choosing the do-nothing scenario means there would be no impact on your organization. In many cases, not taking action can be costly—or could mean that a valuable opportunity goes unrealized.

Reality Check #2: Stop or Go?

Once a specific alternative has been identified, reverify justification and feasibility. The question of justification should have been addressed by performing the financial calculations incorporated into the financial criteria used in the decision matrix. Feasibility can be assessed with greater conviction, since you now know what the solution is. However, if the alternative's feasibility is still in question, several options are available to you. Let's examine some of them.

Market study. If your project is to bring a new product to market, you must determine its market potential. Market research asks customers whether your product satisfies their current or potential perceived needs. This could also refer to an analysis of your target market aimed at determining how much (or how well) your product is differentiated from the competition.

Pilot test. You can try out your project on a small scale, often through the use of a working model of certain project deliverables in a user environment. Sometimes known as *field testing*, a pilot test gives you the opportunity to observe your project's performance under actual conditions.

Trade trial. This is the product equivalent of pilot testing. Here, actual products are introduced into a limited consumer market.

Prototyping. You can build and/or assemble some portion of the project deliverable(s) and put them through performance tests designed to verify whether they meet the performance criteria identified in the requirements. The prototype may be discarded or reused on the project.

Simulation. Computer technology permits modeling of many types of projects. For example, you can predict a product's market potential by analyzing target user demographic data along with assumptions about current and potential needs. Or you could predict the load-bearing potential of buildings, bridges, and vessels through mathematical calculations and computer simulation. The value of simulations lies in their ability to identify potential problems in a risk-free environment.

If the results of a well-conceived and -executed feasibility study indicate that the project should proceed, you can move confidently into the planning and implementation phases. If the results are discouraging, you can use the data to redesign the project and do another feasibility study, and so on, until you've identified a project concept that works.

Third, Refine the Optimum Solution and Develop a Preliminary Project Plan

Up to this point, it's likely that the alternatives—including the eventual best solution—have been defined in a limited way. The description of the preferred solution selected in the previous step may only be a sentence, along with a few qualifying remarks. In Brad's case, the solution statement he is proposing goes like this: "Increase the output of the widget production lines from 600 units per week to 800 units by redesigning components X, Y, and Z," whereas the solution statement he was originally handed read: "Build and install production line #5 in Department ABC; design configuration to be identical to lines 1–4."

THE DILEMMA OF DEFINITION

CAUTION

One of the seemingly inescapable chicken-and-egg situations common to the process of defining a project has to do with how well (to what extent) an initiative—or an alternative solution—is described in the early part of its life. Organizations are often reluctant to invest a large amount of time and money in defining or developing plans around something that they later abandon. The challenge is to spend a sufficient amount of time defining an effort so management can make a high-quality business decision, but not so much time that a large amount of waste is generated from an abandoned project.

Your solution statement must now be converted into an action plan, which can be accomplished in two steps. The first step consists of describing the preferred project solution in detail, including the approaches to and methods of implementation. This requires development of a *Project Definition Document*. The second step consists of developing a *Preliminary Project Plan*—one that can be used to provide a high-level, yet reasonably reliable prediction of cost, schedule, resources, and risks.

Prepare a Project Definition Document

Use the Project Definition Document to elaborate the preferred project solution. This document is the formal "response" to the Project Requirements Document. There are other terms for the Project Definition Document, including *Project Objectives Statement, Project Scope Statement,* and *Statement of Work Document.* Whatever name may you use, the goal is the same: to fully define the work to be done. You'll use it as the basis for all future planning documentation.

The Project Definition Document serves many purposes:

- It identifies what work will be done and how it will be done.
- During planning, it forces stakeholders to agree on the boundaries of the project scope.

- During execution, it helps you identify changes that fall outside project boundaries and that therefore require renegotiation of the original project "contract."
- It helps to establish the completion criteria on which all parties can agree.
- It helps to establish success criteria on which all parties can agree.
- It helps the team agree on the approaches and methods to use.
- It facilitates widespread understanding of what the project will not include.

Although the Project Definition Document's primary purpose is to describe the work, the document may include other information to make it more comprehensive. Normally those items are carried over from the project proposal phase described earlier.

> **KEY TERMS** **Project Requirements Document Versus Project Definition Document** Project Requirements Document and Project Definition Document are the names used in this book for these two important documents. Your organization may use different names. Whatever the names, the intent of the documents is what's important. Use one document—the Project Requirements Document—to capture problems, needs, and opportunities; use the other—the Project Definition Document—to define and describe the project solution. In addition, the order and sequence of these documents is critical—problems must be thoroughly understood before initiating the search for a solution.

A comprehensive Project Definition Document includes these elements:

- **Brief description of the problem, need, or opportunity.** A relatively short, high-level summary of key points made in the project requirements document. It reminds the reader what the original issues were.
- **Proposed solution.** Generally, this is the project title and a brief description of what is deemed to be the best way to address the problem, need, or opportunity.
- **Statement of work and strategy for execution.** The main focus of the document. It's a narrative delineation of the work to be done and a description of how it will be done. The delineation must be stated in sufficient detail to support the development of a detailed project plan (see Chapter 9). The description may describe how certain work ele-

ments are interrelated or provide a high-level perspective on the desired sequence of major work elements to be carried out.

- **Major deliverables.** Lists and describes all the project's outputs and end products. The level of detail in this section could vary from a general description of major outputs to a list of performance specifications of individual project deliverables.
- **Completion criteria.** A description of what must be accomplished, built, developed, or delivered to enable agreement across all stakeholders that the project is complete (different stakeholders may have different interpretations of *complete*).
- **Statement of risks, uncertainties, and unknowns.** Identifies missing data, information, or facts. It may inhibit the team's ability to accurately predict the final project outcomes (cost, completion date, or deliverable quality) as it focuses on missing or conflicting information. The statement ordinarily emphasizes areas where the project may be negatively impacted relative to stakeholder expectations.
- **Assumptions.** Ordinarily take the place of missing information. They represent anticipated values or conditions that may or may not be known to be true or readily verifiable. Assumptions are directed primarily at project deliverables or the methods used to produce deliverables.
- **Project stakeholders.** A list of individuals and organizations involved in the project or affected by the activities and/or outcomes.
- **Success criteria.** The methods that will determine how well the project objectives were met. The criteria should list the critical success factors and quantified levels of achievement.

OBTAIN FORMAL AGREEMENT ON PROJECT DEFINITION   SMART

Treat the Project Definition Document as a kind of "contract"— even if you're managing an internal project. Secure a formal sign-off from as many key stakeholders as possible. When individuals display their formal agreement in advance on what is to be done **MANAGING** and how, they are less likely to offer resistance during project implementation. More important, they are less likely to inflict changes on your project.

Develop a Preliminary Project Plan

The Preliminary Project Plan includes a variety of high-level planning documentation, such as preliminary cost and schedule estimates, a procurement strategy, and an organizational chart of the project team that displays the functional areas to be involved. Since these are not fully developed plans and estimates, present all estimates in terms of ranges. Indicate confidence levels where it makes sense to do so to show that any information you provide reflects your level of knowledge at this stage of the project.

You'll find this plan to be one of the more challenging points in the project's life span. In Chapter 3, we discussed the gap between the certainty desired by management and the inherent uncertainty of projects. This is often the point at which that gap is greatest. You're about to make a specific project proposal to management, who will crave precise numbers.

TRICKS OF THE TRADE

HEDGING AGAINST UNCERTAINTY

In the preliminary planning stage, particularly when making a proposal to management for formal approval and authorization to proceed, consider these tips:

- Recognize that single values and numbers could suggest a level of knowledge (and therefore precision) that is misleading, based on your lack of detailed information about the project.
- Instead, provide estimates in terms of ranges of possible outcomes. For example, instead of saying the project will cost "$475,000," say the project costs "will be somewhere in the range of $440,000–530,000." Instead of saying that "the completion date is October 12," say that the project "will be completed in October"—or perhaps even "in the fourth quarter" if you're facing high levels of uncertainty about the project.
- Expect to encounter resistance and dissatisfaction when you offer ranged estimates. You must be prepared to counter these objections with a discussion of what specific information you lack at this time. (This approach helps management better understand and appreciate the concept of unknowns and uncertainty on projects.)
- Keep any graphics that you produce relatively simple. Detailed graphics suggest a higher level of knowledge or precision than you possess.
- Make clear that any documents you produce are preliminary. Savvy project managers stamp *DRAFT* on preliminary documents.
- Seize any opportunity to alert management and other stakeholders that your levels of precision and confidence at this point are not high, due to a shortfall of information.
- To be fair and appropriate, provide ranges that are proportional to what you don't know. Never use excessively large ranges as a way to ensure that you won't be wrong.

You won't be able to provide the desired level of precision, because you simply don't know enough at this point. You've done a limited amount of analysis, so you can't predict an outcome with much confidence. The unknowns are discussed in Chapter 10.

The schedule you produce in your preliminary planning should be simple and not too detailed. In fact, the level of detail in all your documentation should reflect your level of knowledge and certainty. In most cases, you could only indicate the major phases of the program and identify some high-level milestones. Again, indicate a completion date and a cost estimate in terms of realistic ranges, not specifics.

Figure Out Who Can (and Will) Do the Work

Before presenting your project proposal to management—and as part of your preliminary planning—gain some assurance that the labor and materials required for the project will be available in the event that you get formal management approval to proceed. Nothing is worse than trying to manage a project without the proper resources. It's common to begin the process by searching for internal resources (people who work within your organization). In many organizations, outsourcing or subcontracting is considered only after it has been shown that internal resources cannot satisfy your need. Here are the key questions to ask (in this order):

- Do we have people with the necessary expertise to do the work?
- Are they willing to commit to doing the work, barring any scheduling problems?
- By going outside the company, would we achieve a better result such as a lower cost, higher quality, or faster delivery?
- What are the concerns associated with going outside the organization such as confidentiality and safety?

You can also conduct a preliminary Make-or-Buy analysis, which helps to determine whether it's better to obtain a deliverable or group of deliverables from within the company or from an outside source. A Make-or-Buy analysis should examine this issue from three perspectives:

1. **Perform direct cost comparisons.** Normally cost is the primary consideration in a Make-or-Buy analysis. Comparing costs should be fairly straightforward and the calculations relatively routine.

2. **Consider critical factors.** There are many factors beyond dollars and cents. Consider the attributes of the group providing the deliverables, such as cost, delivery, quality, reliability, and so forth. These factors can be included in a Weighted Factor Scoring Matrix. This approach may include any number of factors.

3. **Apply appropriate filters or constraints.** Certain conditions might exist that would eliminate a given choice—make or buy—even if that choice is feasible and/or cost effective. Here are some examples of filters or constraints (some might call them *show stoppers*):

   - Specific legal concerns
   - A need for confidentiality
   - The need or desire to maintain direct control
   - Significant excess capacity existing in your organization
   - The inadvisability of outsourcing the function

Fourth, Formally Launch the Project

OK, let's review. We've identified the true need, determined the best way to satisfy that need, described how we're going carry out the solution, and developed a sense of how much the solution will cost, how long it will take to carry it out, and who will work on it. At this point, some sort of formal authorization and/or funding approval may be required before the project can proceed.

Make a Proposal for Management Approval

As a project manager, you'll have to present proposals or recommendations to management, and this will be one of your first opportunities to do so. As a guide to making any presentation to management, I recommend using the format below. It may not be necessary to include all this information in every presentation, but using this guide will ensure that you've covered all the key elements of a solid presentation. And taking the time to fully develop some detail for each area in advance makes the presentation go more smoothly and puts you in a position to answer any questions.

- **Needs statement:** A brief description of the need.
- **Background:** A more detailed description of the need, how it was dis-

covered, how it developed over time, and why it's important to the company or organization.

- **Recommended action:** A description of the proposed project initiative or activities that would appropriately address the need, including a description of alternatives considered and why they were rejected.

- **Benefit:** A narrative description of all benefits associated with taking the proposed action.

- **Action risk:** Any negative impacts associated with taking the proposed action.

- **Inaction risk:** Any negative impacts associated with not taking the proposed action.

- **Costs:** An estimate of the range (minimum, maximum, most likely figure) of anticipated expenditures if the proposed action is taken.

- **Cost savings:** An estimate of the range (minimum, maximum, most likely figure) of the dollar savings to be achieved if the proposed action is taken.

- **Schedule:** An estimate of the range (minimum, maximum, most likely figure) of how much calendar time would be needed to implement the recommended solution (note that this is *not* a completion date!).

- **Metrics:** A description of how the quality of the final results will be measured and a description of what will be measured, monitored, or tracked during implementation.

- **Unknowns and uncertainties:** Missing information regarding the issue and actions; generally focused on things that could negatively affect the outcome.

- **Assumptions:** A description of what was used in place of the missing information.

- **Constraints:** Anything that limits or precludes successful implementation of the recommendation.

- **Required support:** The resources needed to implement the proposed action.

- **Liaison:** List of other organizations or people that must be involved for successful implementation, with a description of what's expected of each.

- **Impact on others:** A description of the impact of the proposed action on other organizations, specific individuals, and other programs or activities.

- **Sponsorship:** The level of active and visible support by management or specific individuals necessary to ensure achievement of the stated benefits.
- **Critical success factors:** Any issues that could make or break the project and a statement of what's required to minimize or eliminate any threats.

Secure Formal Authorization to Proceed

You may need to secure formal management authorization at this point to proceed with the project. This ordinarily consists of the formal sign-off on one or more of the key project documents that have been developed thus far. In some organizations, formal authorization is secured on a document called the Project Charter.

The Project Charter design can vary, but most will have these elements:

- A description of the project and its stated objectives
- Anticipated team membership
- The level of authority to be granted to the project manager
- Anticipated project outcomes
- Customers and stakeholders
- Preliminary planning information
- Formal management signatures

Project charters are useful because they do a good job of consolidating relevant project information into a single document. If your organization does not currently use a Project Charter, you could create one of your own.

Conduct a Team Kickoff Meeting

Following the organizational procedures described above to launch your project, you should conduct team-oriented activities. Among the most valuable and usual of these activities is the project team kickoff meeting. The formal kickoff meeting is intended to recognize the "official" formation of the team and initiation of the project execution. The timing for this event depends on when your team members are assigned and when you are perceived as having a full team. Kickoff meetings are a convenient time to review (or develop) mutual expectations, energize the team through presentations from management, and rapidly promote team cohesion.

The Unspoken Imperative: Evaluate the Political Environment

The process outlined above includes most of the formal procedures required to get your project started. If you're a savvy project manager, however, you're also sizing up the political climate that surrounds your project. Here are the basics:

Size up your stakeholders' stake. Once you've identified all the project's stakeholders, take that process one step farther and identify who stands to gain (or lose) if your project succeeds and who will gain (or lose) if your project is deemed unsuccessful. It can be of value to understand and appreciate the nature of everyone's stake in your project.

Identify whose support will be needed. Identify who is in the best position to help and support your project.

Identify who is likely to work against you. Identify the parties who may feel threatened by your project or who, for whatever reason, would prefer that your project not succeed.

Secure a project sponsor. Identify someone in management who can serve as a project sponsor. *Sponsors* are typically members of management who have a significant amount at stake in the success or failure of your project. Sponsors can work through political issues that are beyond your sphere of influence.

Address unrealistic targets or constraints. If your estimated project targets—specifically schedule and cost—exceed management expectations, you may be forced into a situation where you're pressured into accepting unrealistic cost, schedule, or other targets. If this happens, I urge you to pursue some combination of these four tactics:

1. **Respond with a well-developed, data-driven analysis that predicts a different set of outcomes.** Use data to make the case as to why the imposed project targets are unrealistic. This may not get you a reprieve from being expected to comply with unrealistic targets, but it's worth a shot.

2. **Include your original cost and schedule targets in any documents you publish.** Once you publish documents that only show the unrealistic targets, you've sealed your fate and doomed yourself to project failure.

3. **Communicate your professional opinion on "realistic targets" on an ongoing basis.** You must do this without being disrespectful and without appearing angry or bitter.

4. **Be patient!** If your estimates were accurate and valid, the forecasted outcomes that you provide during the project will gradually creep closer to your original predictions (stated in more direct terms, you will eventually be vindicated). Avoid the temptation to gloat.

Key Documentation Used in the Project Definition Stage

In this stage of the project implementation life cycle, the business need is further clarified and the need for a project is recognized. Client needs are documented and the best solution is determined. That solution is defined in detail and a preliminary project plan is developed. A proposal is submitted for formal management approval and, if approved, the project is formally launched. We discussed several of the key documents used to accomplish these critical project steps. Let's review those documents, all of which are illustrated in Figure 6-3.

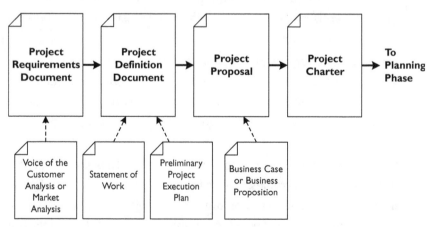

Figure 6-3. Key documents in the project initiation phase

Project Requirements Document. Also referred to as the *Client Requirements Document,* this is the most fundamental document of any project, as it forms the basis of project identification. This document describes and quantifies a problem, need, or opportunity. You can structure it in any number of ways, but it should include the elements described earlier in this chapter.

Voice of the Customer Analysis or Market Analysis. Voice of the Customer (VoC) refers to the process of capturing customer or user input, and is a key input to many project requirements documents. The VoC approach uses interviewing techniques to better understand what the customer needs and desires or to solicit input on opinions, perceptions, and preferences. Figure 6-4 shows an example of a simple VoC questionnaire. You may or may not choose to use this specific approach. However, the results of any meetings or interviews with customers or user groups should be fully documented and maintained for reference by the project team and other interested parties. In lieu of a VoC analysis, a marketing study may be performed; the key difference being that a marketing study doesn't focus on interviewing as the sole source of customer input.

Project Definition Document. The Project Definition Document is the response to the Project Requirements Document. While a project require-

What would you like to have in a _____?
What concerns would you like to share?
What comments or recommendations do you have for improvement?
Why did you mention _____?
Why is this _____ important to you?
What does that _____ do for you?
What problems do you have with _____?
What works well about _____?
What doesn't work well about _____?
What would work better than this _____?
What is missing in the _____?
If you were to design/redesign the _____, describe its
features, performance, _____, _____.

Figure 11-3. Sample Voice of the Customer questionnaire

ments document describes a problem, a Project Definition Document describes the solution. It, too, is a foundational project document that can be constructed in various ways. It should contain the specific elements described earlier.

Statement of Work. While I previously referred to the Statement of Work as a section within a Project Definition Document, many organizations choose to use it as a stand-alone document. It is a narrative document that describes the proposed solution and outlines in limited detail the work to be done. It often lists the major project deliverables, the general approach or methods for doing the work, and how success will be measured. It is the "what" component of the project definition.

Preliminary Project Execution Plan. While the Statement of Work describes what is to be accomplished, the Preliminary Project Execution Plan describes how it will be accomplished. This precipitates the creation of a high-level, or *rough order of magnitude* (*ROM*), project plan. This is the first version of the plan and typically includes a schedule, cost estimate, preliminary resource plan, and many of the components that the final project plan will incorporate. The key difference is that preliminary project execution plan is assumed to be relatively imprecise.

Project Proposal. It's likely that you'll have to prepare some sort of proposal for management approval. You can construct this proposal in several ways, but it should include the elements listed earlier in this chapter.

Business Case and Financial Analysis (updated). As mentioned in Chapter 4, many companies prepare a business case document. Ordinarily a key document when initiating a project, it describes, from a business perspective, the impact the project is expected to have on the organization. At the beginning of the project definition stage, the financial analysis will undoubtedly incorporate the use of relatively crude (imprecise) values. Now that the project is well defined, the values are better defined. Whether or not you are heavily involved in producing this version of the business case and financial analysis, you must secure a copy, make sure you understand it, and keep it in your project file.

Project Charter/Project Authorization Document. You'll probably have to seek formal management approval before you and your team can proceed to detailed planning. As described previously, a Project Charter is the term commonly used to describe the document that constitutes the formal authorization to proceed.

Manager's Checklist for Chapter 6

☑ Identifying a project manager early can add considerable value to the project process. Project managers can help in defining and quantifying customer needs, determining optimal solutions, gathering project requirements, preparing project proposals, writing project business cases, and a host of other activities done in the early stages of project initiation.

☑ While solution-jumping—the tendency to take action before adequately analyzing a problem, need, or opportunity—offers an appearance of decisiveness, it can be harmful in projects, as it sometimes results in the waste of time, money, and resources if the solution is later found to be ineffective.

☑ Identifying the customer's true need—the most fundamental problem or opportunity—is the first and most important step in the entire project process.

☑ Two key documents in defining projects are the Project Requirements Document and the Project Definition Document. The Project Requirements Document details the problem or need; the Project Definition Document details the solution.

☑ A Weighted Factor Scoring Matrix, or decision matrix, is an excellent method for selecting "the best" among several alternative solutions for addressing a customer's needs.

☑ While you won't necessarily need to assign specific resources to your project before it is formally launched, you should try to ensure that sufficient resources will be available, should your project be approved.

☑ Conducting a formal project kickoff meeting is an excellent way to signal everyone that the project was approved, and is officially under way; it will also provide a head start in promoting team cohesion.

☑ Be sure to size up the political climate within your organization. Consider whether any political or cultural issues are likely to impact you or your project.

Building and Maintaining an Effective Team

rad decided to act on his suspicions about solution-jumping—and the information and insights he uncovered in his brief conversation with Milt, the Operations representative. Brad also had a productive meeting with Monica, the engineer responsible for installing the production lines four years ago. With some additional investigation, another working session with Monica, and the input of others around the company, Brad established that the optimum approach to address the need for additional production capacity is to modify the four existing lines so they are able to produce 800 units per week.

In fact, his proposal is overwhelmingly approved after he demonstrates how this solution is better than the one that was handed to him. In addition to providing greater output than the original solution, it would cost considerably less and be done much sooner! Although it took a little digging, cost a little time, and got him involved in a couple of testy conversations, Brad realizes that it was worth it.

As he settles into his new role as corporate hero, it occurs to Brad that he needed the support of many people just to get his project pulled together, presented to management, and approved. The support he'd gotten from these people made him recognize that he wouldn't get far into planning and implementation without the help of those people—and many more. All at once, it hits him: now that his project is officially approved, it's time to form his planning and execution team—fast!

The Mechanics of Building a Team

Some project managers in Brad's situation are tempted to immediately start moving forward on their own. They try to advance the project as far and as fast as possible, seeking the support of individuals only when they can't go any farther. As we'll soon see, this approach may offer the promise of a quick start and appear to save money, but it's probably not a sound long-term strategy.

When Should You Form Your Team?

This is a difficult question to answer, because (you guessed it!)—it depends. The "big bang" approach—where the entire team is formed in a single maneuver—doesn't ordinarily make sense. Two or three iterations of soliciting team members are often needed before the final team composition has been established (very small projects may be the exception to this). As with many aspects of project management, the answer that's right for you will depend on the careful balancing of several competing issues. Here are some useful tips for forming your project team.

Don't try to define the project alone. You simply will not know everything necessary to define any project—even if you might think you do. A more compelling reason to include others is one of the truisms of project work (actually, it's human nature): the less a person participates in defining and planning his or her efforts, the less likely he or she is to take "ownership" of them. And success is greatly enhanced when participants take ownership. So if you define and plan the project alone, team members may feel like they're executing *your* plan, not theirs. Performance can suffer when this happens.

The appropriate team members will become apparent during project definition. In many cases, the people who helped you during project definition will represent excellent candidates for team membership, due to the project-specific knowledge they developed while helping you. In addition, they will probably appreciate an opportunity to finish what they started.

CONSIDER HAVING "INTERNAL CONSULTANTS" ON YOUR TEAM SMART

Most of us tend to think of resources as being either entirely "on" or "off" a project. In the early stages of a project that employs internal resources, this could make the process of getting people formally assigned to work on your project a tricky proposition, **MANAGING** due to two opposing issues. First, the prevailing mindset in many organizations says that you should try to "keep the cost down until we figure out whether we have a project or not." If you're keeping track of hours or costs, having several people formally assigned to your project (and potentially charging large amounts of their time) is contrary to the goal of keeping investigation costs down. Conversely, getting people formally assigned to projects that aren't yet a sure thing can be challenging.

Consider internal consulting as an alternative to formal assignment. Negotiate directly with appropriate subject matter experts or prospective team members. If possible, agree on a deliverable and a cost (the number of hours to be charged to your project). Tie the two together. By doing this, you're less likely to be surprised by excessive labor charges.

You balance the expense of their involvement against their anticipated contribution. Having an individual formally assigned to your project team can sometimes be like hiring an employee. That individual is now authorized to begin charging his or her time to your project. If you're in an environment where costs are tracked and closely scrutinized, you cannot afford to have people "hitting your project" when they're not yet productive. Regrettably, this sometimes happens once employees are being charged to your project. One solution is to develop some relationships that more closely model consulting rather than full-time employment.

Who Should Be on Your Team?

The answer to this question depends—in this case, on the size and complexity of your project.

Medium and large projects in most functional organizations tend to rely on the *core team* concept. These kinds of projects often require work to be performed by several functional areas (departments) within the organization. In the core team model, the objective is to obtain a knowledgeable representative from each functional area needed to execute your project. This representative will serve as your single point of accountability for all work performed within his or her department or work group.

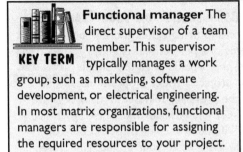

Functional manager The direct supervisor of a team member. This supervisor typically manages a work group, such as marketing, software development, or electrical engineering. In most matrix organizations, functional managers are responsible for assigning the required resources to your project.

On smaller projects, it makes more sense to examine the major elements of work to be done. You should then try to recruit team members according to how well their particular skills match a given element of work.

Whatever the size of your project or anticipated team configuration, it's likely that functional managers (department heads) will be viewed as the resource providers.

Ordinarily, you would approach any given functional manager and provide him or her with information about your project. You would describe the type of competencies that would best satisfy your need. If it's a group you've worked with before, you'll probably have a specific person in mind for the assignment.

In an ideal world, the resource assigned to work on your project represents the optimum match of your needs and his or her skills. Unfortunately, it doesn't always work out that way.

TRICKS OF THE TRADE

GETTING THE RESOURCE YOU WANT, PART I

If you have a specific resource in mind, be prepared to "fight." Prepare a strong argument—in advance—to explain why you need a particular individual. Be sure that there's a compelling functional basis for your argument. Simply saying, "I like working with Sally" or "Joe and I get along well" is unlikely to sway the resource provider.

All too often, you'll get somebody who happens to be available at the time. To be blunt, you may get offered a person who tends to be less in demand, often due to inferior skills or an undesirable behavior pattern. In other words, everyone wants the best resources—that's why they're often overloaded and unavailable.

If you believe this could happen to you, here's a recommendation: establish a climate or tone in which the functional manager—rather than the individual assigned to your project—is viewed as responsible for the success of that department's contribution to the project. Say, for example,

"I'll get back in touch with you right away if problems arise," or "I'm going to put your name down in the Responsible column for this effort." Resource providers who may be willing to accept some responsibility this way may be more inclined to provide a more qualified employee for your project—

GETTING THE RESOURCE YOU WANT, PART II

If you have a specific person in mind, you'll need to make that very clear as soon as possible—and definitely before a specific individual has been named. Getting a functional manager to change his or her mind after he or she has assigned a specific individual to your project may be next to impossible.

and pay more attention throughout the life of your project.

In all of the above scenarios, we've assumed that you'll use people who work in your organization. However, at times it may be necessary to use external resources. The expertise you need may not exist in your company, internal resources may not be available when you need them, or it may make better sense to look outside. Before using external resources, consider these thoughts:

- A competitive bidding process may be required.
- Finding a qualified consultant or contractor can be challenging.
- It's not as easy to direct the efforts of an employee from a different company.

SCREENING CANDIDATES FOR YOUR TEAM

There's no secret recipe that will guarantee a successful project team. However, asking the following questions will help you identify those who may represent the best candidates for a given role:

- Does the candidate have the knowledge and skill to do the job, including technical, problem-solving, and interpersonal skills?
- Does the candidate have the desired personal characteristics for the job?
- Does the candidate believe in the project's goals and seem likely to willingly support them?
- Does the candidate have the time available to provide an appropriate level of project support?
- Is the candidate compatible with other team members who have been identified or are under consideration?
- Does the candidate regard participation on your project as an important function or as an intrusion on his or her "real job"?

- You will need to write and maintain contracts.
- Some "resource flexibility" may be lost (e.g., what happens if the project is cancelled or put on hold and you have a contract with an outside company?).

Identifying Who Does What

As mentioned above, individuals join your team with the general expectation that they represent a good "functional fit" and are able to do the required work. It's up to you, however, to ensure that the duties you give them throughout the project reasonably match their skills. If you ask team members to stretch too far beyond their abilities, they may tend to "shut down" and difficulties will ensue. Conversely, if you grossly underuse their talents (as least from their perspective), performance problems may also result, such as loss of interest, procrastination, and a lack of effort.

As the project's overall scope of work becomes better defined, you can identify more specifically what each team member will do. Eventually, each person's responsibilities will be displayed on a Responsibility Assignment Matrix. (We cover this in Chapter 9). As you move forward, it's important to allow each team member to play a leading role in defining his or her specific work on the project.

Developing a project organizational chart (sometimes known as an *organizational breakdown structure*, or *OBS*) for your project team is an easy way to help everyone understand their roles and responsibilities. A sample OBS is shown in Figure 7-1.

JUST FILL IN THE BLANKS

You can use the organizational chart as a guide and template for team formation. Begin by thinking about all the functional work groups that are needed to contribute their expertise to ensure

TOOLS successful project implementation. Then as specific individuals are assigned to your project, you can add their names.

Team Leadership Starts on Day 1!

As Brad will soon find out, managing the project team begins immediately. From the moment that people are assigned to your project, you're responsible for ensuring that they're heading in the desired direction.

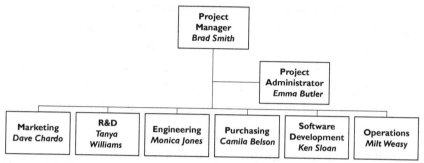

Figure 7-1. Team organization

This often requires tact and influencing ability. Since you're in a matrix organizational environment, you have no formal authority over them, so you've got to be able to lead appropriately.

Anticipating Team Members' Questions and Anxieties

One of the biggest problems that a project manager faces in the early stages of the project is managing the anxieties that newly formed teams can develop. If left unchecked, this anxiety can inhibit early team growth and the development of relationships, thus affecting work output. With that in mind, let's examine some of the more common questions you can expect to be asked by some team members.

What's in it for me (WIIFM)? This question is likely to cross the mind of nearly every individual on your team. Some will wonder about the effect that participating on your project will have on their career. Others will wonder if working on your project is likely to be personally or professionally rewarding.

What will be expected of me? This issue surfaces most often when team members are unfamiliar with your leadership style or approach. The source of this anxiety may pertain to aspects of the role that have little to do with their project tasks. They may be more concerned with issues such as how much personal freedom they'll have, whether you're the type of leader who will micromanage them, or the extent of administrative, clerical, and other undesirable duties you will expect them to perform.

What will your team be like? Many will want to know who else will be on the team and the likelihood that their relationships with other team members will be harmonious. They'll have questions about the team composition. Will the team be unified, or will members tend to bicker? Will everyone on the team be qualified, or will there be some members who will have to be helped along? Will all members be peers, or will there be an implied (or real) hierarchy? This is a legitimate concern, as some of the most dysfunctional teams are those that have an organizational manager as a team member. Inevitably, rank surfaces as an issue—directly or indirectly.

Addressing Team Members' Questions and Anxieties

Generally speaking, you can reduce or eliminate many of these anxieties by having a conversation with your team. Specifically, call a team meeting as early as possible to cover the following topics as openly and honestly as you can:

- Review the project objectives (the true need) and justification for doing the project (benefit to the organization).
- Review the project proposal (the solution) and why that represents the preferred approach.
- Bring up any problems or constraints they may have to deal with as a team.
- Clearly define the role of all team members in terms of their functional contribution (use the organizational breakdown structure).
- Honestly characterize your leadership style (free and open, trusting, exacting, etc.).
- Describe your expectations regarding project logistics (frequency and timing of team meetings, for example).
- Describe your expectations in terms of behaviors, such as team meeting conduct or preferred methods of communication.

In addition, you may want to meet individually with each team member to discuss the following aspects of their involvement on the project:

- The reason why they were selected
- Any unique expectations you may have of them
- Any problems or constraints they may encounter
- Any apprehensions that they may have about you or the project

How Teams Evolve and Develop Over Time

There are various models that describe how teams evolve throughout the life of a project. One of the more popular models suggests that teams pass through four distinct stages.

1. Forming. In this stage, people are gathering information about the project. They're concerned with what they'll have to do, who's on the team, how they'll fit in with the others, how your leadership style will affect them, and many other issues related to starting a project.

2. Storming. In this stage, team members react to what they've learned during the forming stage. They decide how much they like the project objectives, their roles and responsibilities, and the demands you've placed on them. Incidentally, they're also deciding how much they like you and your leadership style.

3. Norming. This stage is only entered if the conflicts that arose during the storming stage were properly handled. In this stage, team members become reconciled with the project and their role on it. They focus on the work to be done. Behavioral norms are developed and team members begin to know what they can expect of others.

4. Performing. In this stage, work becomes routine. Team members interact well and produce high-quality results. All members understand one another's responsibilities and behavioral patterns. They work well together in solving problems, making decisions, and communicating with one another.

BEWARE OF THE FIFTH STAGE!   SMART

Some have enhanced the popular model above by adding a fifth stage. It occurs at the end of the project and is often called the *Mourning* or *Adjourning* stage. Expect the team's output and efficiency to slow down during this stage. Some team members may **MANAGING** have moved on to other assignments—hopefully only after completing their work. The remaining members may become preoccupied with what is going to happen to them once the project has ended. A subset of the initial team may have to scramble to complete the last few tasks, which may not have been included in the original project plan. The fifth stage really tests the project manager's leadership skills.

Adapting Your Team Leadership Style for Each Stage

As the team evolves, so should your leadership style. Flexibility is one of

DON'T BE A TASKMASTER

CAUTION During the forming stage, some project managers are anxious to get off to a good start by having team members immediately roll up their sleeves and get going on their respective tasks. This approach—which overemphasizes the work—can be dangerous, as it ignores the social aspects of team evolution. Some people need time to get to know one another and become comfortable interacting. If you don't provide this opportunity, communication may be stifled, thus decreasing the team's effectiveness. This can be particularly problematic on long-term projects, where members need to work together for a long while.

the most valuable assets you can possess. The concept of flexible leadership works for both teams and individuals, as we discuss later in this chapter. Here's how the models suggest adjusting your style to meet the demands of each stage described above:

Forming. In this stage, your team is looking to you to provide information, organization, structure, and context. Accordingly, you adopt more of a structuring/directing style. Make sure everyone understands the project and the project environment, such as deliverables, objectives, and justification, your expectations of them as team members, and the processes and procedures to be followed.

Storming. The potential for conflict is greatest in the storming stage. You cannot simply direct the team through this period—but you also cannot ignore the conflict as it surfaces. To do so would threaten your ability to lead your team into the next stage, and you'll remain mired in conflict. A guiding/coaching style works best during this stage, as you take the necessary time to address the team's questions, concerns, and sometimes their challenges of your course of action. Be sure to explain your decisions during this difficult period.

Norming. In the norming stage, your direct involvement should diminish considerably as team members chart their course by laying out their work. Encourage them to participate more actively as you adopt more of a supporting/encouraging style. Individual team members should assume personal ownership for their part of the project. Without this feeling of ownership, it will be difficult to advance to the next stage.

Performing. This is a great stage for you as project manager. Your role becomes less stressful. You assign basic responsibilities and let team members take the lead in determining the best way to carry them out. You may allow them considerable decision-making authority as you assume a delegating/facilitating style. In this stage, you're primarily an enabler. Confident in your team's abilities, you manage by exception, concerning yourself primarily with variances from the intended course of the project.

Mourning (or Adjourning). In this stage, much of your project's original structure has disappeared or become irrelevant, as your team members struggle to figure out what they need to do to conclude the project successfully. Now you return to more of a structuring/directing style. Adopt a strong leadership style as you organize the remaining work, assign specific responsibilities, and provide direction so you can avoid the never-ending project syndrome.

Getting the Most from Your Team

As project manager, you provide leadership at two levels—with the team as a unit and with each individual on the team. Though there are many similarities, each has unique considerations. Let's begin by examining some of the more important leadership issues that pertain to the team.

It Takes More Than a Pizza Party or Rock Climbing to Build a Team

Team building is one of the more misunderstood principles in project management. Many people equate team building with the poorly orchestrated, "voluntary" social gathering or the artificial, imposed, often hokey events. Though some of these approaches work, they often evoke more laughter than respect, for one reason because it's difficult to pull them off without appearing contrived.

The core concept of building a team is simple: people who spend time together get to know one another better and therefore feel more comfortable working together. Although you can certainly do this by taking the team out to lunch, meeting after work, or organizing a social gathering, it doesn't necessarily have to be done in a nonwork setting. You can also do it in ways that tie members together and tie everyone to the proj-

SMART MANAGING

TEAM EVALUATION

Consider having your team take some time out periodically to evaluate how well you're functioning as a team. This activity offers several potential benefits: it will help you address areas of concern before they grow, provide you with insights on potential areas of self-improvement, and get team members to interact outside the confines of the project tasks.

ect. The most effective team building occurs when the team members expand their knowledge of each other and the project at the same time. Here are some examples:

- Develop mutual expectations between the project manager and the team.

- Develop a project network diagram by using sticky notes on the wall.

- Develop a code of conduct for project team meetings.

- Work together to design a major senior management status report.

- Celebrate significant project milestones together (e.g., design approved, first unit shipped, etc.).

Recognizing and Addressing Differing Perspectives

Numerous instruments are available for characterizing personal preferences, thinking processes, communication styles, and other aspects of personality. Though the instruments differ considerably, the principle behind all of them is the same: *people are different from each other.*

This unsurprising fact has two major implications for you as a project manager. First, individuals must be managed as individuals. (We explore that aspect later in this chapter.) Second, every member of your team is likely to have his or her unique perspective on just about everything. Although this isn't news, you should continually bring it to the team's attention. Most conflict arises from differing opinions, which are

MISTAKE PROOFING

INCLUDE CONFLICT RESOLUTION TRAINING

Because we all look at things differently, conflict among team members and between your team and you is inevitable. Conflict leads to personality clashes and other unproductive outcomes. Include conflict resolution training as a part of your training and development plan. Urge others on your team to do the same.

rooted in our differing perspectives. Drawing attention to these simple realities helps team members understand that conflict is inevitable and helps reduce the anxiety that conflict creates. It also helps you channel conflict in a way that produces stronger, synergistic outcomes.

The Value and Purpose of Team Meetings

The most common team meeting is the regularly scheduled status review. This is where you're likely to conduct most of your formal project business. However, regular team meetings have other purposes beyond the obvious technical and logistical ones. Meetings remind your team members that they're not working alone and they must rely on one another. Team meetings also serve as the primary forum for growing the team's *collective intelligence*. This term refers to a subtle dynamic that occurs at each team meeting: everyone on the team learns a little bit more about the project and each other's contribution. This is one of the more underrated benefits of team meetings, and it's worth specific mention.

From time to time, some members of your team may ask to be excused from one or more team meetings because they are not currently engaged in executing project tasks. In deciding whether to approve their request, you have to weigh the value of their presence (in terms of growing the collective intelligence) against their perception that you're wasting their time. It might be more appropriate to consider the extent to which their absence may affect team cohesion and synergy.

CONDUCTING EFFECTIVE TEAM MEETINGS

One of the primary reasons people dislike team meetings is because they're poorly conducted. Here are a few simple rules:

- Publish a meeting notice in advance, with agenda items and anticipated time allocations.
- Start and finish the meeting on time.
- Don't repeat everything for latecomers.
- Release everyone as soon as business has been conducted.
- Cancel a meeting if you believe there's nothing new to discuss.
- Limit the meeting to project management issues; don't allow it to be a forum for a few members to hash out detailed design decisions, for example.
- Publish brief meeting notes that emphasize action items; highlight those due by the next meeting.

SMART

MANAGING

Managing the Interfaces

Fledgling project managers often make the mistake of assuming that their primary role is to direct the team's day-to-day actions. This approach is guaranteed to enrage experienced team members. It also overlooks a key aspect of team leadership. One of your most important responsibilities is interface management. You're the only person in the organization responsible for ensuring a healthy working relationship between and among the project team members. And it's unlikely that all of the desired interactions will take place without your support and involvement. Your role in fostering teamwork and synergy may require you to devote some energy to actively managing interaction among team members.

You should encourage team members to interact whenever the need arises and discourage them from waiting until the next team meeting to address any issues or concerns they have with one another. Waiting wastes time and opportunities. However, you also need to know what's going on, so make sure that team members keep you informed whenever they take important actions or make important decisions.

What About Rewards and Recognition?

This is one of the most difficult aspects of a project manager's job. Although philosophies and approaches to rewards and recognition vary widely, you should consider two simple points relative to this important topic.

1. **Rewarding your team reinforces the team concept.** Some organizations claim to support teamwork, but they recognize and reward individual performance. This sends a mixed message and undermines teamwork. If you reward and recognize teams and teamwork, the greatest contributors may feel slighted, but it's still the best way to show that you value teamwork. Your projects are more likely to succeed when your team members work together to succeed as a team.

2. **Rewarding individual heroics promotes undesirable behavior.** When organizations (or project managers) develop a reputation for continually rewarding the individual hero, they risk setting up an environment of competition within the team. Even worse, they may be encouraging some individuals to undermine the efforts of their teammates as a way to inflate their own importance.

Getting the Most from Individual Team Members

Savvy project managers recognize that team leadership is more than just managing the team as a unit—it also involves managing the one-on-one relationship with each team member. Let's examine some of the key aspects of managing the individuals on your team.

What People Need to Do Their Job

You can't expect your team members to effectively carry out their duties unless they have certain basic information, such as:

1. A clearly stated objective (for the overall project and for their specific tasks)
2. The purpose of each objective (the value or benefit)
3. Direction and guidance on accomplishing each objective (plans, processes, and procedures)
4. The skills required to do the job (and what to do if some skills are absent)
5. The tools and resources required to do the job (and how to acquire them)
6. Feedback on their performance (and how it will be delivered)
7. A description of their limits of authority (what they are allowed to do or to decide on their own)

Strive to ensure that each team member understands these basics throughout the life of the project. You may have to be proactive, as you cannot always rely on team members to bring deficiencies to your attention. In some cases, they may not even be aware of their own deficiencies.

Establishing Mutual Expectations

Among the most productive and powerful things you can do as a project manager is to establish a set of mutual expectations between you and each individual team member. This will help solidify and clarify your working relationship. Some of the more common expectations are listed in Figure 7-2.

The expectations listed in Figure 7-2 are generic. You should expand this list to include expectations specific to your project, your particular situation, and each individual team member.

Project Managers Expect Team Members to:	Team Members Expect the Project Manager to:
■ Be committed to the project	■ Stimulate group interaction
■ Provide accurate and truthful status	■ Promote participative planning
■ Follow the project plan and defined processes	■ Define all relevant work processes
	■ Define performance expectations
■ Be proactive	■ Manage conflict constructively
■ Take direction, but push back appropriately	■ Share information appropriately
	■ Remove obstacles
■ Propose actions that make sense	■ Insulate team from unproductive pressures
■ Communicate/inform proactively	
■ Be accountable for decisions	■ Resist unnecessary changes
■ Respect other team members	■ Recognize and reward achievement
■ Maintain a positive attitude	

Figure 7-2. Developing mutual expectations

Informal Leadership

Although most project business is conducted through formal means such as team meetings, savvy project managers recognize that more important business is often conducted through informal means. This leads to the concept and practices of *informal leadership*.

It is beneficial to visit team members in their workplace occasionally or to call team members from time to time just to see how things are going. It'll help you maintain good relationships, show your interest, and offer an avenue of information that may help you run the project more effectively.

> **SMART MANAGING**
>
> **DISCRETION IS IMPORTANT**
> Meeting informally and privately with individual team members provides opportunities to discuss issues openly and frankly. To get the most accurate, reliable, and valuable input, you must establish an environment where team members can speak freely and honestly. You must never violate their trust by divulging sensitive information given to you in confidence during these one-on-one sessions.

One caution: you must carry out your visits for the right reasons, in good faith, and for the obvious purpose of enabling you to manage the project better. If you chat just to get one team member to tell you about another, for example, the strategy will quickly backfire. Also, if your interest in team members is insincere, it will probably show.

Note: Not All Team Members Are Created Equal

One of the best methods for getting the most from individual team members is to treat them as individuals. There are several models that describe the principle of *flexible leadership*. One popular model suggests that a project manager can consider a two-dimensional matrix comprising the work to be done versus the readiness of an individual to successfully perform the work. Models like this are useful in the optimum style when interacting with any given individual team member. The styles that most leadership models suggest are similar to the four team leadership styles (structuring, guiding, supporting, and delegating) described above.

You should individualize the principles of flexible leadership even more than this. Recognize that people have individual needs that may require an approach that goes beyond the four leadership styles. Be aware, however, that truly managing individuals as individuals requires insight and intelligence—and courage. You need to determine what motivates each individual on your team and then provide it whenever you can and whenever it makes sense to do so, but in ways that don't show favoritism.

If you do show favoritism, some people will ask why you're treating someone differently. You need to display a reasonable and fair-handed explanation.

I once worked for a person who had the ability to treat people as individuals and could do it fairly. As a result, the people in his work group would consistently give their all—and more. Why? Because they recognized that he truly cared about them as individuals—and they didn't want to let him down.

Manager's Checklist for Chapter 7

☑ Despite the popular vision that the team magically comes together at one time and begins work, the reality is that team members trickle onto your team as you realize your needs.

☑ Err on the side of getting members assigned as soon as you can, rather than "waiting until there's more definition." Their participation in defining the project is likely to reap benefits in the form of greater commitment to the project's success.

☑ If there's a specific person you want on your team, prepare an argument as to why you need that person. Make sure you put your request in before the assignment is made—resource providers aren't ordinarily inclined to reverse a decision once they've made it.

☑ Don't be afraid to "screen" candidates who have been assigned to your project. Confirm that their qualifications, attitude, and track record make them suitable for the job. If you have concerns, voice them early and factually.

☑ Members of newly formed teams will have questions, concerns, and anxieties. Address these issues early in the project, before they turn into problems. Conduct an open team meeting and review the project, your expectations, and your project leadership philosophy. This is likely to answer many of their questions or concerns.

☑ As the team evolves and matures, team members will become increasingly self-sufficient, requiring less direct involvement on your part. Adjust your leadership style over the course of the project according their rate of growth.

☑ Good team leadership recognizes that everyone is different. This suggests that trying to manage everyone on the team in exactly the same way is flawed thinking. Don't be afraid to manage individuals as individuals.

Managing the Project Interfaces

Brad had not been a project manager long before he realized that he wouldn't get far alone. He assembled the project team that had helped him tremendously as he navigated the early stages of the project investment life cycle. As he contemplates what lies ahead—the detailed planning of his project—two more thoughts about project life cross his mind.

First, he thinks about the amount of work that was needed to launch a project the right way. "Well worth the effort," Brad says to himself. He feels confident that he is managing the right project.

His second thought comes immediately on the heels of assembling his core project team. It's the recognition that his core team is only one of many groups that he will have to interact with by the time Project Apex is done.

You will be in exactly the same situation with your project. One of the most important things you can do as a project manager is recognize that interfaces are a big part of project life. Your project—like Project Apex—doesn't exist in a vacuum. And like Brad, neither will you as the project manager. The right time to think about what the project interfaces are and how you will interact with them is now—before you get into detailed planning and execution. Addressing interfaces later—as you bump into them along the way—may lead to some unpleasant surprises and impede your ability to manage them effectively.

Some interfaces you'll encounter may exert considerable influence on your project—and their influence may not be favorable if they're not properly handled. Learning how to recognize and properly deal with project interfaces can have a profound effect on the success of your project and on your level of heartburn.

As we're about to learn, it's unlikely that you'll have much control over these interfaces. But you can identify them, learn to understand them, work with them, and adapt to them. In short, you can *manage* them.

This chapter helps you do that effectively.

What Are Project Interfaces?

Consider for a minute that you and your project are at the center of everything. Experienced project managers will tell you that this view of the world is far from reality—but it enables us now to take a productive perspective on the concept of project interfaces. Figure 8-1 shows some of the typical points where you and your project come in contact with the outside world.

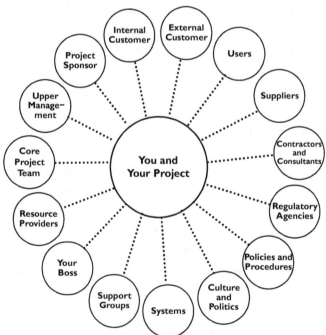

Figure 8-1. A project manager's outside interfaces

Note that some of the interfaces in Figure 8-1 are people. People interfaces are usually called *stakeholders*. Technically, stakeholders can be something other than people (a department, for example), but it's easier to consider stakeholders as the people component of project interfaces. Let's examine who these people are and what makes them so important to you.

What Makes a Stakeholder a Stakeholder?

While *stakeholder* is a common term in project management, it has many interpretations. So rather than trying to develop a single definition, it is helpful consider the characteristics of stakeholders. We list several here. Any one or more of these characteristics makes someone a stakeholder when he or she:

- Stands to gain (or lose) through the success (or failure) of the project
- Provides funding for the project
- Has invested resources in the project
- Participates in (works on) the project
- Is affected by the outputs of the project
- Is affected by the outcome of the project
- Is in the "chain of accountability"

All of these characteristics are probably clear, except perhaps the chain of accountability. It is worth specific mention, due to its political implication. The *chain of accountability* is often found in complex matrix organizations where a number of departments exist, each with layers of management. In these types of organizations, several formal signatures may be required before a project (or major decision) is considered approved. Everyone who signs off on the project approval is viewed as being in the chain of accountability. Accordingly, they see themselves as stakeholders and feel they have the right to exert influence on the project if they sense the need. Politically astute project managers pay close attention to these people.

What Do You Need to Know About Stakeholders?

Stakeholders can be in any department or at any level within the organization. You'll constantly interface with stakeholders throughout the life of your project, leading us to another critical consideration: what do you need to know about stakeholders to properly manage your relationship with them? Here some of the key things you should learn about project stakeholders:

Who they are (by name). Don't be content to recognize that certain groups of people (such as functional supervisors) are stakeholders. Figure out who every individual stakeholder is—by name.

The nature of their stake. What do they stand to gain if you succeed? Or lose if you fail? How much? In what way? Does the outcome of the project affect them professionally or personally?

What they expect from you. You can best find out what they expect by meeting with stakeholders individually. Since this is time consuming, you may want to limit face-to-face meetings to key stakeholders, such as clients or management sponsors. If there are differences between what they expect and what you believe they should expect, you must resolve those differences immediately.

What you expect from them. Some project managers have difficulty expressing their expectations to members of senior management, as they don't feel they have the right to tell managers what to do. Bear in mind that stating expectations to senior manager does not mean that you're telling them what to do or how to act. You are simply describing what you need to be successful in managing your project.

> **SMART MANAGING**
>
> **GET TO KNOW THEM**
>
> The more you know about an individual stakeholder, the better your chances for developing and maintaining a strong and beneficial relationship with her or him. Cultivating good professional relationships with stakeholders may help you in ways you can't envision at the outset of the project.

Their priorities. Priorities can be expressed many ways. Among the most important priorities you need to be aware of are the relative importance that any given stakeholder places on the four elements of project success and control that we discussed earlier in the book: project schedule, project cost, deliverable performance, and deliverable quality. Try to gain an understanding of which element(s) are most important to key stakeholders, such as the client and management sponsor.

The rules of engagement. This item pertains primarily to the mode of communication and, in particular, your personal interaction with a given stakeholder. It's probably most relevant to your interaction with members of management. For example, you should consider what form of communication a particular manager prefers—formal or informal; written or verbal. It's best not to guess. Don't be afraid to ask, "If an incident were to occur, would you prefer that I phone you right away and follow up with a detailed memo, or write you a memo and call you later to discuss the situation?" For some senior managers and executives, these are not trivial issues.

Whether they are friend or foe. For a variety of reasons, your project may not be universally loved and supported. Think about whether any given stakeholder is more likely to support you and your project—or to undermine your efforts. This issue is closely tied to the nature of the person's stake, as there may be situations where a stakeholder is adversely impacted by the existence (or success) of your project. Think about this in conjunction with that stakeholder's ability to exert influence over you and your project. So, for example, if an individual isn't supportive but has little impact over you or your project, you probably don't need to spend much time worrying about that person or trying to change his or her mind.

Internal Stakeholders and Their Roles

Let's begin our examination of stakeholder groups with internal stakeholders—people within your company or organization. One thing that makes internal stakeholders particularly important is that the *perceived success* of your project is often judged by the *perceived satisfaction* of internal stakeholders. Even though you meet the prescribed project targets and run the project efficiently, if certain internal stakeholders form an unfavorable opinion of your project, your image will still suffer.

Let's look at some of the key stakeholder groups—who they are, your relationship to them, and how they can affect you and your project.

Internal Customers

Customers are the people for whom you're doing the project. *Internal customers* are people within your company who have a particular need that your project will address. The internal customer often pays for the project and receives the benefits (business impact) and/or project deliverables. Project Apex is an example of an internal project: the Operations department that Brad has been interfacing with is his internal customer.

The Project Sponsor

The *project sponsor* (also called *management sponsor*) is not ordinarily a specific organizational position; it's a role played on a project, typically a representative of upper management who has a large stake in the outcome. The sponsor helps you when you don't have the connections or the clout to make things happen. Having a management sponsor is particularly valuable when you are faced with problems, issues, or situations beyond your sphere of influence. Sponsors facilitate approvals or decisions, assist with resource assignments (or reassignments), and serve as advisors and mentors to you as you manage the project. A good sponsor also helps you overcome political and organizational obstacles. Make sure you keep your sponsor fully informed about your project.

SMART MANAGING

Go Out and Get a Sponsor If You Have To!

A project sponsor is an invaluable asset to you and your project—particularly if you work in a matrix environment and your project is large or complex. If a sponsor is not formally identified, go out and get one! Seek out a member of management who has a high stake in the success or failure of your project. Ask if he or she would be willing to serve as the project sponsor. Be prepared to describe the role and your expectations, if he or she asks. Many times, you will find people to be willing; if they have a large stake in your project's outcome, they will want you to succeed.

Upper Management

Your organization's senior management may or may not be directly involved in your project, but it's the ultimate stakeholder. What if all your organization's projects were dismal failures, wasting large amounts of money and other resources for little or no business results? Upper management would be perceived as incompetent. If you're assigned to manage a critical or high-visibility project, upper management may wish to play an active role. Hopefully, its involvement will be positive and not lead to unnecessary or unproductive meddling or micromanagement—two of the project manager's greatest aggravations.

The Core Project Team

Many people will work on your project, perhaps dozens if your project is large. In many cases, however, you'll be directly and immediately assisted by a small group of people—the *core project team*. In most matrix organizations, several departments or work groups are needed to complete the project. Your life as a project manager is simplified if your core team comprises a single representative from each participating department or work group.

STRIVE FOR SINGLE-POINT ACCOUNTABILITY

TRICKS OF THE TRADE

In multidisciplined environments, several people from each of several departments will work on your project. In situations like this, assemble a core team that consists of a single representative from each participating department or work group. Strive to create an environment where people are not merely department representatives, but people who assume responsibility for coordinating the work done by their departments. This *single-point accountability* reduces the number of interfaces you must maintain, ensures you always know whom to contact, and greatly reduces or even eliminates the finger-pointing that can come when multiple parties are responsible.

When a clear-cut departmental model is inappropriate for constructing the team, core team roles are likely to be determined by the nature of the work. As major work elements are identified, shrewd project man-

---

SOME TEAM MEMBERS MAY NOT BE GOOD STAKEHOLDERS

CAUTION

A word of caution about the role of team members as project stakeholders: As discussed in Chapter 2, some organizational cultures fail to create a strong sense that project excellence is important; these cultures tend to reward functional excellence, not project excellence. If this sounds like your organization, your core team members might lack a strong sense of commitment to the project's success. They know that as long as they do what their boss expects, they'll be OK—despite how the project turns out. Be aware of this possibility and manage these situations accordingly.

---

agers seek out the person who's best equipped to perform that element of work most effectively and efficiently.

Functional Supervisors (Resource Providers)

In matrix organizations, it's common for project managers to "borrow" resources from other departments. Your team members are, in essence, representatives of the managers who control those resources. You might think that this kind of relationship would cause those managers to have a strong stake in your project's outcome. For a variety of reasons, though, that isn't always the case. By gently reminding functional supervisors that the people they assign are a reflection on them and their group, you may be able to build a stronger stake. You should also strive to build a good long-term relationship with resource providers. If your relationship is good, you may be able to acquire better resources.

Your Manager (or "Boss")

Nearly all project managers report to someone. For simplicity, I'm going to use the term *boss*. Even though your boss may not be directly involved in your project, he or she is still a stakeholder. Take Brad, for example, and his boss, Gina. If Brad manages Project Apex poorly, it will reflect poorly on Gina because she assigned him to manage the project. More important, Brad is acting as Gina's *agent* (similar to our discussion on functional supervisors above). That's still the way most organizational hierarchies are interpreted—and it's a key concept that you need to appreciate. Your boss, therefore, has a very big stake in you and your project. This implies that you have certain responsibilities.

One of the biggest is to keep your boss fully informed at all times. Your boss will view one of your primary responsibilities as protecting him or her from being blindsided—being surprised or embarrassed due to a lack of critical information or knowledge that you failed to provide about a situation or change, for example.

Support Groups

Various groups within your organization—such as Legal, Accounting, and Clerical Support—often play a role more supportive than active, depending on your specific needs. This leads to a difficult decision: should you make supporting groups part of the project core team or not?

This can be a tough call. Having a group representative on the core team and attending regular team meetings promotes team cohesion and enhances the "collective intelligence" we discussed in Chapter 7. However, if their role does not call for ongoing, regular involvement, representatives may feel you're wasting their time. This is an issue you should discuss with each individual at the outset of the project. Their contribution—whatever its magnitude—is likely to be richer if they participate at a level that you're both comfortable with.

External Stakeholders and Their Roles

By definition, *external stakeholders* are people involved in the project but not part of the organization. Although they normally want your project to succeed, their stake is often focused on their own interests. This is true of most external stakeholders, except those for whom you're doing the project (external customers). Most external groups—particularly those supplying goods and services—are inclined to take a parochial view of your project. This means that you cannot always count on them to put what's best for the project ahead of what's best for them. This may sound cynical, but it's reality.

External Customers

Projects that address the needs of *external customers* (*stakeholders*) are typically characterized by contracts, so project managers normally have a clear idea of the customers. Usually the biggest challenge with external customers is getting them to articulate their needs in a clear and useful way—that isn't continually changing. Although unclear objectives may be a problem with internal customers as well, the stakes are higher with external customers because there are contracts—sometimes with fixed dollar amounts. In addition, some external customers have

LEARN ABOUT THE LEGALITIES!

SMART MANAGING

If you believe you will be leading many projects that involve external customers, make sure you develop your knowledge of the legal aspects of project management. This may extend from understanding contract law to how you are expected to conduct yourself when interacting with clients. Many good books and training courses cover these subjects.

the attitude that because they're paying the bill, they have the right to change their minds about what they want. Whether that's philosophically true is irrelevant; the important point is that such a view of the world can make life difficult for you. So, be attentive and take precautions.

Users and User Groups

User groups are a special case of external customers, primarily when you're developing or producing a product that's marketed and sold to outside consumers. I like to think of user groups as *latent stakeholders*. In most cases, they don't realize that they're stakeholders, as they're probably unaware of your project and the products it creates until those products are released into the marketplace. You must often act as a surrogate stakeholder by asking key questions about users' likes and dislikes, preferences and choices, and so forth. The organization's Marketing department may play the role of surrogate user, so projects that involve user groups often necessitate maintaining a strong interface with Marketing.

Suppliers

Nearly all projects require materials that must be obtained from outside companies. Finding reliable suppliers of high-quality products can be difficult, though. This is one reason why many companies adopt *preferred supplier programs*. Make sure you know whether your company has such a program. In principle, these programs attempt to forge long-term, cost-effective relationships with high-quality suppliers.

Unfortunately, you cannot always count on quality; preferred suppliers are often determined more by cost than by quality. And you should never assume that you can rest easy because you're using a preferred supplier. In fact, you should never get complacent with any supplier relationship or agreement. A common mistake made by project managers is assuming that suppliers do not require much of your personal attention because you have a contract or purchase order in place. You should monitor and control suppliers as much as any other individual or group working on your project.

Contractors and Consultants

Much of what was said about suppliers holds true for contractors and consultants. The main difference is that you're purchasing labor or services instead of materials. You should be aware of two big issues with this group of stakeholders.

First, contractors and consultants will probably feel less of a stake in your project than any of the stakeholder groups. The extent of their stake rarely goes beyond their body of work and their image. After all, protecting their image is vital to their survival. It's unlikely that they would do something that would jeopardize their image—even if it were the right thing to do for your project. Harsh? Yes. Reality? Yes.

Your second concern relates to purchasing services if you aren't familiar with a particular contractor or consultant. Because talk is cheap and glossy brochures are easy to print, you must be cautious when engaging a contractor or consultant. Whenever possible, use performance-based criteria and a verifiable track record when selecting these stakeholders.

Other Interfaces

Most of your interfaces will be stakeholders. However, there are other entities you will interface with, so you need to be aware of them and know how to manage them.

Regulatory Agencies

Regulatory agencies (such as OSHA and EPA in the United States) are not identified as stakeholders for a reason: in general, the people in these agencies are uninterested in your project. The extent of their concerns is to ensure that you behave as you're supposed to—namely, according to their laws or rules. Many project managers sidestep any involvement with this interface group. If you do that, you may be taking a risk. Your best bet is to cooperate with regulatory agencies, as they often assess penalties that far exceed what you may save by avoiding them.

A common mistake that project managers make with regulatory agencies isn't avoiding them, though—it's simply forgetting to involve them. A very important thing to keep in mind with regulatory agencies is that they have one thing that you don't—power. And lots of it.

Organizational Policies and Procedures

This is an important interface. As a project manager, you're expected to follow the organization's policies and procedures. That's just one of the unspoken expectations of project managers in most organizations. So you'd better be familiar with the policies and procedures relevant to your project.

One dilemma you're likely to face is whether to abide by those you disagree with. (And it's likely that you will disagree with some!) You should not disregard policies for purely personal reasons—it's bad for your image. Often the only justifiable reason for disregarding policies arises when not following them is beneficial to project success; ensuring the success of your project is your highest duty to the organization.

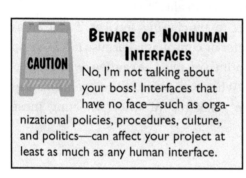

BEWARE OF NONHUMAN INTERFACES

CAUTION

No, I'm not talking about your boss! Interfaces that have no face—such as organizational policies, procedures, culture, and politics—can affect your project at least as much as any human interface.

Systems

There are many organizational systems. Most are process oriented and computer based, internal to the organization, put in place to help the organization function more efficiently. Examples include the labor-charging and payroll systems, data processing systems, procurement or purchasing systems, inventory-tracking systems, manufacturing systems, and possibly even project management systems in the form of scheduling, cost reporting, or resource logging. You need to understand which (if any) of these systems are relevant to your project. As with policies and procedures, you're ordinarily expected to use the systems in which your organization has invested so much money.

Culture and Politics

This interface has been mentioned many times throughout this book—for good reason. A project manager who does not understand (or chooses to ignore) the impact that an organizational culture or political environment may have on his or her project is destined to a life of mediocrity at best. You need to be aware of cultural and political elements, seek to understand them, and strive to work with them. The following questions may help you.

- How does my company feel about project management?
- How do various groups (or specific managers) feel about project management?
- Who are the real decision makers in any given situation?
- What kinds of results tend to get positive recognition and rewards?
- Why do these two departments dislike each other?
- Which members of management can make things happen, and which have limited power?
- What can I get away with?
- What will cause me to get punished?
- What types of behaviors and attitudes are valued?

It's important to point out that being politically astute is not the same as "sucking up." Being *politically astute* means that you know whom to go to in case of trouble, you understand the boundaries of appropriate risk-taking, you are aware of who will support you and who won't, and you strive to keep key players informed.

Special Considerations in Interface Management

In addition to identifying, understanding, and properly handling specific interfaces, a few special interface issues merit your consideration.

Managing the Management Interface

It probably goes without saying that this particular interface is important to your future. The way you deal with organizational management forms the basis of their impressions of you and your potential for advancement in the organization.

Interfacing with managers—upper management in particular—is challenging at times. They'll continually provide input, direction, and feedback throughout the project. Unfortunately, not all managers will consider your personal and interpersonal needs as carefully as you consider the needs of those you direct. Consequently, you may receive input, feedback, and direction:

- When you aren't expecting it

▪ In a form you may not comprehend

▪ That you disagree with or you feel is in error

▪ With little explanation or justification

▪ Without concern for your buy-in or commitment

▪ Without regard for your feelings or self-esteem

▪ That you may find personally or professionally offensive

What can you do in negative situations like this? Always maintain self-control, while ensuring that communication channels are open and clear.

The shaded box below offers some general suggestions for dealing with these kinds of negative interactions—and a couple of positive ones. As is true with situational leadership, your ability to vary your style and react appropriately is vital to maintaining a healthy, long-term relationship with the management interface.

When reacting to negative feedback:
- Ask for clarification on anything you don't understand.
- Don't bluff; admit if you don't know the answer.
- Don't lie.
- Don't blame the situation on other people or circumstances.
- Don't promise anything you know you can't deliver.
- Correct misconceptions tactfully.
- Confirm your intention to investigate any complaints.
- Don't react emotionally.

When reacting to positive feedback:
- Share praise liberally.
- Don't be too self-effacing ("really, it was nothing," "I guess I lucked out").

Developing Mutual Expectations

One of the most beneficial but neglected activities in project work is taking the time to clarify mutual expectations with stakeholders. Many people assume that they'll automatically know what the other parties are going to do, how they'll behave, and what they'll deliver. Yet many situations exist where the project ends, and one or both parties are disappointed.

When expectations are not clarified, the results can be finger-pointing, rework, poor working relationships, misunderstandings, and dissatisfaction.

Figure 8-3 lists several examples of basic expectations between a project manager and four critical stakeholder groups. Use these as starting points for discussions with specific stakeholders on your next project. Work with stakeholders to expand each list to include project-specific expectations.

A customer usually expects the project manager to:	The project manager usually expects a customer to:
■ Understand the customer's business ■ Understand the customer's priorities (cost/schedule/quality/performance) ■ Be able to look at things from the customer's perspective ■ Keep the customer fully informed of progress and changes	■ Always speak in terms of needs, not solutions ■ Articulate requirements in the process as early as possible ■ Actively participate in the requirements process ■ Provide the information, data, and insight necessary to do the job ■ Minimize changes during the project
Upper management usually expects the project manager to:	**The project manager usually expects upper management to:**
■ Assume total accountability for success of the project ■ Abide by the limits of authority and control that have been granted to the role of project manager ■ Keep them fully informed of project status and changes through informative, concise reports ■ Alert them as soon as it becomes evident that any prescribed project targets cannot be met	■ Define expectations, including project and individual performance, limits of authority and autonomy, etc. ■ Set reasonable and achievable targets and goals ■ Openly and formally affirm support for the project to all appropriate managers and organizational members ■ Arbitrate/resolve counterproductive political infighting
Functional supervisors usually expect the project manager to:	**The project manager usually expects functional supervisors to:**
■ Articulate resource needs clearly and in enough time to react ■ Be sensitive to people's duties outside the project ■ Provide appropriate growth opportunities for their people ■ Keep them informed of project status and changes	■ Supply the "right" talent for the job ■ Minimize project disruptions through continual reassignments ■ Serve as a spokesperson for his or her project to upper management

Figure 8-2. Mutual expectations (continued on next page)

The project manager's boss usually expects the project manager to:	The project manager usually expects his or her boss to:
■ Involve him or her in appropriate aspects of the project ■ Develop a regular project status-reporting format and frequency that meets his or her needs ■ Keep him or her fully informed proactively ■ Protect him or her from getting blindsided	■ Support his or her in the face of problems ■ Help negotiate politically oriented issues, particularly high-level or organizationally sensitive ones ■ Serve as a spokesperson for his or her project to upper management

Figure 8-2. Mutual expectations (continued)

Understanding Your Position of Power

One aspect of project leadership for which many project managers should develop a keen appreciation is their position of power relative to any given stakeholder. When trying to determine the best way to interface with that stakeholder, you will often find yourself in one of three power positions. Let's examine these three positions and how they relate to your life as a project manager.

Position #1: You have the authority. People in a position of authority are able to produce a preferred outcome without relying on others. They can order (and get) what they want. This situation is common in the military, but rare for project managers. In some matrix organizations, however, project managers are perceived as having a small amount of *implied authority* over team members and some support groups.

Sometimes, the amount of authority is defined in the job description for the project manager role. Authority can also be implied through management behavior—for example, do senior managers typically support decisions made by project managers? Even if you sense that you have some authority, you must guard against overusing it as this may lead to feelings of resentment by those working for or with you on the project— and to the perception that you are an ineffective leader. Some project managers may be granted a certain amount of implied authority by team members (and others) through a phenomenon referred to as *expert power.* People believe in the project manager because he or she has con-

siderable knowledge or special technical, administrative,
or people skills.

Position #2: You must rely on influence. Influence means you need to work with others (or through others) to produce desired outcomes. Influence is most often used when dealing

> **Expert power** The ability to gain support and compliance due to the perception that an individual **KEY TERM** possesses a superior level of knowledge or capability. In other words, people are more willing to do what you ask because they feel you know what you're doing.

with people who do not report to you and is a common form of power in matrix organizations. In this situation, you're perceived as being on the same level of power as those you are working with. Project managers get most things done through this method, making use of influence is among the most important skills you can learn.

Position #3: You should appreciate reverence. *Reverence* refers to the awareness, understanding, and appreciation that you have little or no ability to directly control a particular outcome. This is a common position with respect to your interface with senior managers and executives. When you're in this position, your best response consists of recognizing that, although you cannot determine a particular outcome, you may be able to predict it and plan around it.

Manager's Checklist for Chapter 8

☑ Your project exists within an environment that includes many points of interface.

☑ Any one of a number of characteristics can make someone a project stakeholder. You may have many more stakeholders than you think.

☑ You need to actively manage stakeholder relationships.

☑ Learn as much as you can about every stakeholder. This will help you manage your relationship with them more effectively.

☑ Project sponsors can be very helpful. Go out and find one if one is not presented to you.

☑ Beware of suppliers, subcontractors, and consultants. They typically don't assume a strong sense of stake in your project's outcome.

☑ Nonpeople interfaces—policies, procedures, organizational culture, politics—are key interfaces and just as important and influential as the people interfaces.

Preparing an Integrated Project Plan

B rad leans back in his chair as he finishes his sandwich. Life is good. He believes he already understands the project management process fairly well; he demonstrated that when he came up with a more cost-effective solution than the one Gina had handed him.

And he's proud of the way he was able to work with others in the organization (many of whom are now on his team) to prepare and present a comprehensive business case for his project. "And I got it approved by management in record time," he says to himself and smiles.

Brad looks forward to the challenge of leading his project core team. Suddenly he lurches forward in his chair ... again.

"How am I going to get all of this work done?" He picks up the inch-thick folder containing the documentation he has already accumulated on Project Apex. "We need a plan!"

Brad is definitely on the right track, but he must recognize that his plan needs to mesh the contribution and involvement of several project players, including his team, his customer, his management sponsor, contractors, and many others we discussed in Chapter 8.

What Brad needs to develop is an Integrated Project Plan. Let's give him some help on how to accomplish this.

But First ... Develop a Project Management Configuration Plan

Even if your organization has documented project management procedures, they may not be detailed. Even worse, your organization may have no formalized procedures whatsoever. Either of these situations could hamper your ability to achieve project success.

To reduce confusion and increase control, you should prepare specific guidelines around project management procedures for every project you manage. Think of this set of guidelines as (and call it) a Project Management Configuration Plan—or PMCP. (Note: This is my term; there's no industry standard term for this.) The *PMCP* is a description of how you intend to conduct business from a project management perspective. It is a marriage of good process and good documentation—and an excellent way to communicate your expectations to your team and to other stakeholders.

A well-designed PMCP addresses these (and many other) questions:

- Who should be involved in project planning?
- What approach should be used to prepare cost and schedule estimates?
- What approach should be used to develop the project schedule?
- What planning documents will we (the team) produce?
- How will work assignments be determined?
- What are appropriate and inappropriate channels of communication?
- What will be the frequency of team meetings?
- How will we deal with risk and uncertainty?
- How will progress be tracked?
- What documentation will be used for change control?

Figure 9-1 illustrates a partial checklist of elements that you could incorporate into your Project Management Configuration Plan. As with any other template or form, you'll expand or modify the PMCP to suit your specific project, your organizational culture, your project team members, your organization's existing procedures, and your own management style.

Planning	Execution and Control
General approach	*Progress measurement*
■ Preferred process	■ Methods of measuring
■ Who should be involved	■ Verification requirements
■ Required documentation	■ Required documentation
Scope definition	*Change management procedures*
■ Defining tasks	■ When to report a change
■ Sizing of work packages	■ Required documentation
■ Use of a WBS dictionary	■ Approval limits and procedure
Time estimating	■ Distribution of contingency
■ Estimating effort	*Team meeting guidelines*
■ Estimating duration	■ Frequency
■ Estimating contingency	■ Attendance expectations
■ Preparing a basis of estimate	■ General agenda
Cost estimating	■ Format for status reports
■ Preferred procedure	**Communications/Personnel**
■ Estimating contingency	*Roles and responsibilities*
■ Preparing a basis of estimate	*Rules of engagement*
Schedule preparation	*Mutual expectations*
■ Graphical format	*Review and approval procedures*
■ Use of software	

Figure 9-1. Portion of a Project Management Configuration Plan

The PMCP provides key stakeholders (your team, the customer, and your project sponsor, for example) with a wealth of information on how you plan to manage your project. It is an excellent tool for structuring communication and managing expectations.

INCLUDE EXISTING PROCEDURES   SMART

A Project Management Configuration Plan (PMCP) is not intended to revise or replace your organization's current project management process. Any existing project-oriented procedures should be incorporated into your project's PMCP. Reference them in **MANAGING** your PMCP, and make certain that your team members are familiar with how to follow them.

Identifying What Needs to Be Done (Scope Management)

The first step in the planning process consists of identifying exactly what you're going to do—commonly referred to as *defining the scope of work*.

It starts by identifying the major work elements. These major elements are systematically broken down into progressively smaller pieces, until each piece becomes a comfortable size to estimate, execute, and monitor.

Some Basic Definitions

Here are some of the terms commonly used in scope management:

Activity or Task: Many definitions exist for these two terms. Many use them interchangeably to describe a very small work element. Purists might say that *tasks* are smaller elements of work than activities, but there's no standard for this. *Activities* consume resources. They have a finite length (time) and an expected cost.

Work Breakdown Structure (WBS): The WBS is a graphical tool—perhaps the most foundational tool in the project planning process. It's a tree diagram that displays how major work elements comprise smaller pieces of work (activities).

Work Package: This term has a variety of definitions. Work packages have two basic characteristics:

1. They are logical groupings of related activities that exist within your WBS.
2. They are deliverable oriented—that is, executing all the activities in a work package typically produces some tangible or verifiable outcome, result, or output (called a *deliverable*).

Responsibility Assignment Matrix (RAM): The RAM is a two-axis chart that shows how project work and project stakeholders are related to one another. The RAM correlates specific work elements with specific individuals.

Step 1: Breaking Down the Work

It is virtually impossible to manage all the work needed to successfully execute a project without breaking that work down into manageable pieces (activities). This is the objective behind developing a Work Breakdown Structure (WBS). A fully developed WBS is the starting point in the development of an Integrated Project Plan. It enables you to estimate activity durations, prepare your schedule, estimate activity costs, prepare your project budget, assign responsibility, and carry out several other critical steps in the planning process.

SCOPE—A TALE OF TWO MEANINGS

SMART

MANAGING

The term *scope* has two interpretations that are different in concept. It's important to understand what each meaning represents and how each is applied in discussions you may have. Here the choice of specific wording is important.

Project scope is the term normally used to refer to the overall mission, goals, and objectives of a project. Project scope also characterizes the overall size or extent of what the project will address. For example, building and installing a few storage racks implies a smaller initiative than installing a computer-controlled storage and retrieval system—but each is an expression of project scope. The project scope is ordinarily the focus of the Project Definition Document that we discussed in Chapter 6. In the case of Project Apex, the project scope could be described as "Modify the four existing manufacturing lines so they will be capable of producing 800 units per week."

Scope of work is the term normally used to refer to the individual elements of effort (taken collectively) that must be performed to accomplish the project. These are the so-called tasks or activities—the small pieces of work that are ordinarily done by individuals. The efforts represented by all the items that appear on a project schedule (or in your list of activities) comprise the scope of work.

In an attempt to save time, some project managers bypass the process of structuring and organizing the work and generate a long list of required activities. This is a poor idea. Although it may work for very small projects (20–30 activities with 1–2 people), it does not work well on projects that involve dozens of activities (sometimes hundreds) with multiple project participants and interrelated activities. The chance of overlooking important activities is too high.

What does a WBS look like, and how do you create one?

We look at a simple example to answer that question. Let's say you'd like to host a birthday party in your backyard. As most people would do intuitively, you begin by recognizing there are a number of large "chunks" of things that must be done (these are the major work elements we mentioned before). These chunks are displayed in Figure 9-2. They represent the beginning of the WBS development process and consist of the following:

- The party needs to be carefully planned. (Although this is what we're doing now, it should still be identified as part of the project work!)

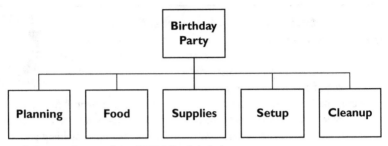

Figure 9-2. Levels 1 and 2 of WBS for birthday party

- The guests need to be fed.
- Supplies (tables, chairs, paper plates, etc.) are needed.
- Some amount of effort is needed to physically set up for the party.
- Some amount of effort is needed to clean up after the party.

You've already begun subdividing the work to be done, and identified Level 2 of your WBS. (Level 1 represents all of the work to be done—the overall project.)

The key at this point is to verify, as well as possible, that you have identified all the major "chunks" of work that make up the entire project. In other words, you must believe that every element of work required to conduct your party will logically fit into one of these five subgroups. Let's assume that's the case. You now proceed to the next level of detail.

Consider the work required with regard to setting up for the party. You will have to clean the pool and clean your house to make them presentable for your guests. You will have to set up some tables and chairs, mow your lawn, and set up a volleyball net. And it would be nice to have music playing during the party.

As you develop this list, you begin to sense that these things can be put into natural groupings of activities, and decide to refer to them as Games and Entertainment, Prepare Home, and Guest Furniture. These groupings are shown in Figure 9-3.

Reflecting on these three categories, you feel confident that everything that you need to do to set up for the party can be placed in one of these groups. However, you do not feel as if you have broken down the work far enough yet. You realize that the grouping called Games and Entertainment is not specific enough because you find yourself asking

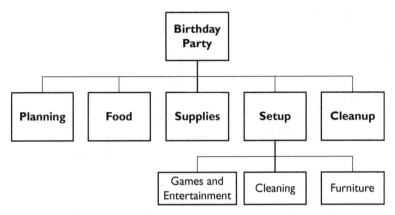

Figure 9-3. Level 3 of birthday party WBS (breaks down "Setup")

questions such as "What games?" "What type of entertainment?" "How much time will it take to set these things up?" and "What will it cost to provide games and entertainment?" You realize these questions can't be answered without additional detail, which triggers the development of WBS Level 4. Once you've done this (Figure 9-4), you feel confident you know what you have to do to set up for the party.

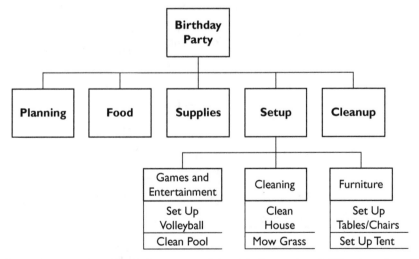

Figure 9-4. Level 4 of birthday party WBS (with "Setup, level 3" broken down)

You continue this thought process with the other major work elements until you've developed an entire WBS to the appropriate level of detail.

So far, you have laid out your WBS in a format that looks like an organizational chart. However, projects are often displayed more clearly when they are organized as a tree diagram. Figure 9-5 shows what the entire Birthday Party WBS might look like in tree diagram fashion.

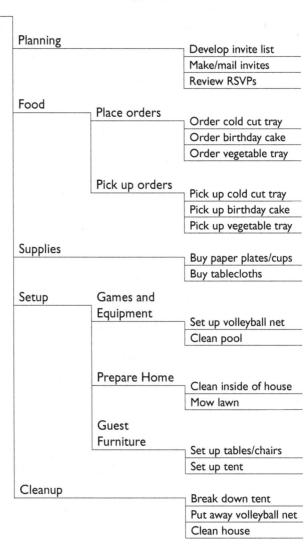

Figure 9-5. Birthday party WBS displayed as a tree diagram

Why Create a WBS, Anyway?

Why take the time and trouble to create a Work Breakdown Structure?

START BY THINKING ONLY ABOUT THE WORK

In the birthday party example, you may have noticed that we weren't concerned about the timing, sequencing, or the cost of activities as we developed our WBS. That's OK. In fact, your only concern when developing your WBS should be to thoroughly identify all work necessary to execute the project. Don't concern yourself with issues such as who is going to do the work, how long it will take, and how much it will cost until you've identified all of the project activities.

Couldn't you just start listing the activities and throw them onto a schedule? Yes, you could. However, without a frame of reference—an organized, logical structure—your chances of identifying all the work elements required to execute the project are close to zero. And you wouldn't find out that you were missing activities until the project was under way. That's likely to cause a major disruption in your timeline—and delay project completion.

Here are several other good reasons why it's smart to prepare a thorough WBS:

- The WBS provides an easy-to-read graphical representation of the work, allowing stakeholders to review it for missing work elements.
- People often underestimate the effort required to execute a project. A fully developed WBS underscores how much work is actually needed.
- The WBS provides a convenient, logical template that you can use to estimate the duration and cost of each activity as well as to assign responsibilities and resources to activities.
- The WBS provides an excellent source for examining the risks associated with the project.

A Work Breakdown Structure forms the foundation for the entire project planning process. As you'll see in the next section, it provides the basis for nearly all other planning steps.

Step 2: Identifying the Dimensions of Work

A properly developed Work Breakdown Structure allows you to identify every single work (activity) element required to complete the project. Once you've done this, you're ready to move forward with the planning process.

For each activity on your WBS, you need to consider important characteristics, which we refer to as the *dimensions of work*. You use these dimensions as input for future planning steps:

- **Scope:** The work that must be done to complete each activity, how it will be done, and what will be produced.
- **Responsibility:** The person accountable (normally to the project manager) for the successful completion of the activity.
- **Resources:** A description of the labor, materials, or supplies needed to complete the activity.
- **Duration:** The window of time within which the activity is expected to be completed.
- **Effort:** The number of days or weeks that resources will actually spend working on the activity.
- **Cost:** How much money will be spent on labor and materials to execute the activity.
- **Quality:** How well the work should be done or how well any activity outputs should perform.
- **Sequential relationship with other activities:** Identification of any other activities that must be completed before this activity can start.

A Nifty Application of the WBS

A well-developed WBS can be used as the basis for a fill-in-the-blank template to capture and display some of the dimensions of work as they become known. Figure 9-6 illustrates this nifty use of the WBS.

Another application of this technique is cost estimating, which is illustrated later in this chapter.

WBS Work Package & Cost Account Numbers			Responsible Party	Effort Required	Resources	Estimated Cost	Precedent Task
Project XYZ $785,000	10X-Design $70,900	101-Mechanical	M. Jones	8 Weeks	2 Designers	$20,500	----
		102-Electrical	R. Smith	6 Weeks	2 Technicians	$18,000	101
		103-Software	H. Baker	10 Weeks	3 Programmers	$32,400	101, 102

Figure 9-6. Using the WBS to capture activity data

Step 3: Identifying Who Does What

The Responsibility Assignment Matrix (RAM) is a tool that displays how project participants interact with project activities. The most common type of interaction is, of course, identifying who is assigned to execute an activity (the responsible party). But the concept of interaction also assumes other forms, such as technical experts who are asked to consult on certain activities, organizational managers who must formally approve the completion of certain activities before the project can move forward, or a client representative who must be notified when certain activities have been completed. The RAM provides an opportunity to document these types of people-project interactions. Figure 9-7 illustrates an example of a Responsibility Assignment Matrix.

WBS Element	Project Team Members					Other Stakeholders		
	I.B. You	M. Jones	R. Smith	H. Baker	F. Drake	Sponsor	Clnt Mgt	Func Mgt
1.0.1.1 **Activity A**	N				R			
1.0.1.2 **Activity B**		R	C					
1.0.1.3 **Activity C**						A		G
1.0.2 **Activity D**			R		S			A
1.0.3.1 **Activity E**			R			N		
1.0.3.2 **Activity F**				R				
1.0.3.3 **Activity G**	R				S	A	A	
1.0.4 **Activity H**		R				C	N	

Key: R = Responsible, S = Support Required, C = Must Be Consulted, N = Must Be Notified, A = Approval Required, G = Gate Reviewer

Figure 9-7. Responsibility Assignment Matrix

Along the left of the RAM are the project activities—a direct output of the WBS. (These should be work elements, not functional responsibilities.) Across the top are the major project participants. These should be specific individuals, but you may indicate department names if specific individuals have not yet been assigned. In each cell is a letter that denotes the type of people-project interaction. There are no standards for the codes—use whatever works for your particular situation and include a key. Here are some possible interactions:

- Responsible
- Accountable
- Must be notified
- May be notified
- Participant

- Document reviewer
- Input requested
- Approval required
- Support
- Gate reviewer

The RAM can be a valuable communication device as it displays the project participants and their implied relationship to one another as well as to the project.

Identifying How Long It Will Take to Do Everything (Time Management)

Once you've identified the work elements (activities), the next major planning step consists of modeling the optimal sequence of activities and estimating how much time will be needed to execute them. Together, these two dimensions enable you to estimate how long it will take to execute the entire project.

The principal output of this step is a *Control Schedule*—an activity-based timeline that the team will use as a map to execute the work and that you will use to maintain proper control of the project and meet the targeted completion date.

Some Basic Definitions

Time management and scheduling involve the use of terminology that you should be familiar with. Here are some basic definitions:

Critical activity: An activity that has no latitude with respect to when it could start or finish. If a critical activity is delayed, the project completion date will be impacted unless some corrective action is taken.

Critical path: The longest path through the project's network (logic) diagram. All activities that lie on the critical path are critical activities. The length of the critical path establishes the time required to complete the entire project.

Duration: The window of time within which an activity is expected to be completed.

Effort: The number of labor hours expected to be spent working on an activity.

Float (or slack): Flexibility, or latitude, with regard to when a specific activity can (or must) be worked on. Activities with float time could start late, but could still be completed on time and not cause a schedule delay.

Forward pass/backward pass: Techniques for calculating the amount of float associated with each activity. Activities with zero float are critical activities.

Milestone: A point in time that marks an important event, such as the completion of a project phase, a major decision point, or the completion of a major project deliverable. Milestones are not activities; they do not consume time or resources.

Network (or logic) diagram: A type of process flow diagram that models the desired sequence of activities. It graphically depicts which activities must be completed before others can begin and which could be done simultaneously.

Parallel relationship: The name given to the condition where two activities could (or should) be executed during the same period of time.

Predecessor activity: The name given to an activity that must be completed before another specific activity can begin.

Series relationship: The name given to the condition whereby one activity must be done before another can start.

It's worth noting that there is almost universal agreement on the usage and definitions of these terms.

Preparing a Project Timeline: An Eight-Step Process

There are many ways to prepare a project schedule, but the systematic, eight-step approach below should serve you well.

Step 1. Prepare for scheduling by identifying schedule activities on the WBS. Using the WBS, identify the specific activities that will appear on your schedule. You should have already broken down these activities to a level where you can track and control their progress. (Remember the 4 percent rule-of-thumb from Chapter 5?) Define each activity in sufficient detail so that all relevant project participants understand the activity completely.

Step 2. Develop the network diagram. Prepare a logic diagram that models the preferred sequence of activities. (Later in this chapter we discuss how to do this.) Proper sequencing of activities is achieved by continually asking these two questions:

1. Which activities must be completed before certain others may begin?
2. Which activities could be done (or need to be done) at the same time?

The secret to minimizing the time required to complete the project is this: minimize the number of series relationships (defined above); in other words, do as many activities as possible in parallel (during the same time period).

Step 3. Estimate preliminary activity durations. Identify how long each activity would take, assuming full-time commitment and unlimited resources. While it's unlikely you will always obtain full-time commitment from resources, starting with this assumption establishes a benchmark of the best possible schedule. You make allowances for resource limitations in step 5. Obtain the estimates from people who are expected to do the work.

Step 4. Calculate specific calendar dates and times. Use the logical sequencing you developed, your preliminary estimates of activity durations, and an assumed start date to position the project timeline on a calendar. Calculate a project completion date, being sure to accommodate holidays, vacations, and other special situations. This first iteration represents the earliest possible completion date.

Step 5. Finalize resource commitments, accommodate resource limitations, and finalize estimates of activity durations. Secure resource commitments

---

TRICKS OF THE TRADE

WHY ASSUME UNLIMITED RESOURCES?

In steps 3 and 4 of the scheduling process, we recommend that you assume the use of unlimited resources when developing the first version of your schedule. The purpose of this suggestion is strategic. This version of the schedule will not be published, and is intended to be used only as a defensive maneuver, if necessary. Here's why:

In today's project environment, project deadlines are sometimes imposed and represent nothing more than the date that someone would like the project to be completed. They're not always realistic, and rarely in sync with the amount of resources you will be able to secure. This version of the schedule will enable you to demonstrate that even with unlimited resources you could not possibly complete the project by the imposed deadline.

and assess resource availability, based on the version of the schedule you developed in step 4. You will have to rework your project schedule (recalculating dates and times) to accommodate resource constraints such as part-time participation levels or specific periods of unavailability. Several iterations may be required before resource availability matches prescribed execution dates.

Step 6. Identify and accommodate external constraints. *External constraints* are immovable calendar dates or time periods that exist outside of your project team and are beyond your control. Examples may include work done by others (unrelated to the project), reliance on owner-furnished equipment, and site availability.

Step 7. Compare the estimated end date and the required end date. Once you've accommodated all constraints, create a baseline control schedule. Document all assumptions and commitments. If your estimated completion date lies beyond the expectations of your management or your client, a *risk-based approach* (commonly called *crashing*) may need to be performed. Several reference publications are available that describe the crashing process.

Step 8. Calculate the critical path and develop a control schedule. Once you've successfully navigated the steps described above, you're ready to identify the critical path (which tells you where to focus your attention during project execution) and convert the network diagram into an easier-to-use format (a Gantt chart or linked bar chart).

Let's now examine some of the key steps in schedule development more closely.

Developing a Network Diagram

Just as some project managers bypass the WBS step, others manage their projects from a to-do list or by placing schedule activities onto a tool such as Microsoft Excel. This is a bad idea. Some projects have complex interrelationships among scheduled activities, and all projects have some amount of dependencies (series and parallel relationships) among activities. It's best to create a model of these relationships with a network diagram.

Network diagramming begins by defining the sequential relationships among the activities you will place on your schedule.

The most common graphical convention for drawing network diagrams is the Precedence Diagramming Method (PDM). *PDM diagrams* consist of boxes that represent activities. The relationship among activities is indicated with arrows.

Figure 9-8 illustrates how a *series relationship* is modeled using PDM. Here, Activity A must be completed before Activity B can begin. This is also known as a *finish-to-start* relationship, for obvious reasons. Series relationships are the most common type of relationship in network diagramming and in projects.

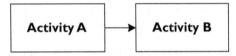

Figure 9-8. PDM series relationship

The other type of relationship occurs when two activities can be done at the same time—a *parallel relationship*. Figure 9-9 illustrates one way of showing a parallel relationship in a network diagram. In this example, Activity C and Activity D must both be completed before Activity E can begin.

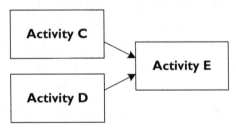

Figure 9-9. PDM parallel relationship

Note that even though activities C and D appear as if they are being executed in the same time frame, no relationship is implied between them, as there is no arrow connecting them.

In situations where it is necessary or desirable to execute two activities simultaneously, use the format illustrated in Figure 9-10. Both represent examples of parallel relationships. This type of relationship links either the start or the finish of two activities.

This is all you need to know to construct your own network diagram!

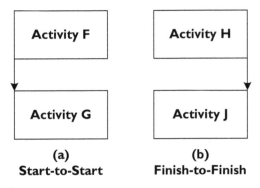

Figure 9-10. PDM parallel relationships

Begin by examining your WBS, where you've identified the activities that you will use to develop your schedule. As you look at each individual activity, consider the interrelationships that might exist between that activity and others by asking these questions:

- What activities must be completed before this activity can start?
- What activities cannot start until this one is complete?
- What activities could be worked on concurrent with this one?

Several methods allow you to capture the information on activity interrelationships. You can construct an ordered list, spreadsheet-style chart (using the WBS), or a wall chart. Using a spreadsheet offers the easiest transition to most scheduling software tools.

How about an example? Let's say that our family is preparing for a ski trip. We might identify a number of activities and their relationships (dependencies) as shown in Figure 9-11. Once again, note that at this point we're not concerned with who's doing the work or how long it will take. Our only objective is to display the logical interrelationships of the project activities.

A STICKY SITUATION!

TRICKS OF THE TRADE
Here's an easy, effective, and educational way to construct a network diagram in "real time." Assemble your entire team in front of a very large wall chart (several pieces of easel paper taped on the wall work well). Put activity titles on sticky notes, one to a sheet. Place activities on the wall in ways that visually display interrelationships: put series activities side by side and stack parallel activities one above the other. When you're satisfied with the general flow of activities (normally left to right across the page), draw the arrows to indicate all dependencies. Before you know it, you have a network diagram—and a team that fully understands how it was developed. This is a powerful team-building activity.

Activity Number	Activity Name	Depends on Activity
1	Prepare picnic basket	4,5,9
2	Awake, shower, dress	—
3	Load the car	1,7
4	Make sandwiches	2
5	Make hot chocolate	2
6	Drive to ski slope	8
7	Gather all skiing gear	2
8	Get gas	3
9	Gather munchies	2

Figure 9-11. Activities and interrelationships for the ski trip

Using these relationships and PDM graphical conventions described earlier yields the simple network diagram shown in Figure 9-12.

Estimating the Time Required to Execute Activities

Once you've properly modeled the logic with a network diagram, you're ready to move to the next scheduling step: estimating how long it will take to get the work done. To accomplish this step, you must consider two forms of time consumption.

The first form of time consumption concerns the number of labor hours that resources will actually be working on an activity. This is referred to as *activity effort*. This also represents the amount of time that

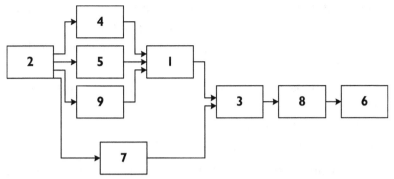

Figure 9-12. Network diagram from the ski trip project

resources will charge to your project, an important aspect of project cost management.

The second aspect concerns the window of time within which the activity is expected to be completed. This is referred to as *activity duration*. The length of time that an activity is displayed on a project schedule is its duration.

Here's a way to think of the relationship between effort and duration: if a resource worked full-time on your project, effort and duration would be the same value, although this is not usually what happens. So if a resource worked, let's say, half-time on your project, the duration would be twice as long as the effort.

Here's where the art of scheduling comes into play. Although we just seemed to describe duration as a calcu-

> **YOU NEED BOTH!**
>
> To properly manage your project, you need to understand, quantify, and track both effort and duration. Since *effort* is the amount of time resources will be charging to your project, it's related to project cost management, which includes cost estimating, budget preparation, and cost control. Since *duration* is the amount of calendar time needed to execute a task, it's related to project schedule management, which includes schedule estimating, schedule creation, and schedule control.

lated value, that's not necessarily the way it works in real life. Duration should be determined by considering the effort required to complete an activity, then making appropriate adjustments based on these considerations:

- The quantity of resources assigned to work on an activity (and how efficiently they can work together at the same time)
- The general availability of the resources (half-time? quarter-time? 10 percent?)
- Specific periods of inactivity or unavailability (vacations, other obligations)
- Weekends and holidays
- Number of hours assumed in each workday

In other words, *duration* is a negotiated figure that represents a meeting of the minds between you and any given resource. And once an agreement is reached, think of that as a kind of contractual relationship—the responsible resource promises to finish the activity within a window of time and you accept that estimate.

ASK FOR THREE ESTIMATING INPUTS

SMART

MANAGING

Whenever resources provide estimates for accomplishing work, ask them for at least these three things:

1. The amount of *effort* (or labor hours) required to complete the activity
2. The *duration*, or window of time, they believe they will need to complete the activity
3. A *basis of estimate*—a detailed description of how they determined both figures, including critical assumptions

You are now well positioned to fully understand how these figures were derived. This helps you verify their validity before plugging them into the project schedule and budget. It also helps you assess variances from plan and helps you recognize and manage any changes that occur as the project progresses.

Converting Your Network Diagram to a Project Control Schedule

While network diagrams are useful for scheduling, they are less than ideal in tracking progress or displaying schedule information to stakeholders. This requires the creation of a Project Control Schedule. A Project Control Schedule is a logic-based bar chart (also called Gantt chart) that has been overlaid onto a calendar. It provides you with all the information you need to monitor progress and maintain control over the project timeline. An illustration of the control schedule for our ski trip project is shown in Figure 9-13 (using my assumed durations).

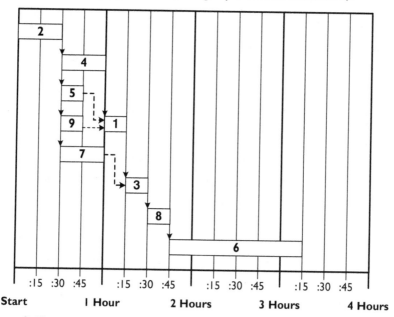

Figure 9-13. Control schedule for the ski trip project

The Project Control Schedule offers a good way to visualize when project resources will be used. This is a good thing, but it might require you to develop one more iteration of your schedule before you're done. Because our network diagram was based primarily on the logical sequencing of the work, it is possible to end up with a situation where a specific task performer may be scheduled to work on several activities during the same period of time. This issue can be alleviated through a technique called *resource leveling*.

Calculating the Critical Path

Once you've prepared your final schedule, you'll undoubtedly begin thinking about how you're going to maintain control and keep your project on schedule. Now is the time to start thinking about the critical path concept. Study the schedule illustrated in Figure 9-13. Do you notice that one set of activities is continuously tied together with no breaks between them? In the ski trip project, the sequence of activities 2-4-1-3-8-6 is the critical path.

> **Resource leveling** A scheduling technique that addresses the problem of overcommitted resources by adjusting the project schedule (typically by extending it). A good example might be
> **KEY TERM** this: imagine that Activity X and Activity Y are two parallel activities both assigned to Joe. Obviously, Joe can't do them at the same time. To fix this, you could model a series relationship between X and Y, and Joe could work on Y after he was done with X. This would extend the schedule. Another option, of course, is to acquire another resource to execute one of Joe's original activities. In that case, the schedule would not have to be extended, but securing extra resources is often a challenge.

    Although the critical path is fairly obvious in this schedule, it's more difficult to see on larger, more complex projects. For these projects, a calculation is required to determine the critical path. You accomplish this by performing two manipulations of the schedule—referred to as a forward pass and a backward pass. The *forward pass* calculates the earliest possible date that each project activity could start and finish without impacting the overall project deadline. The *backward pass* calculates the latest possible date that each project activity could start and finish.

    Figure 9-14 illustrates how these calculations could be applied to a simple network diagram.

    Let's begin with a description of the graphical conventions shown in the

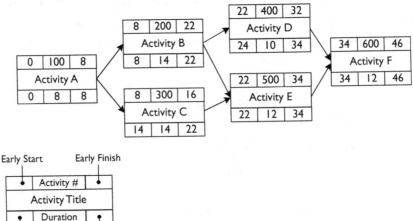

Figure 9-14. Calculation of forward and backward passes

lower-left corner of Figure 9-14. The four key scheduling attributes of activities described above (early start, early finish, late start, late finish) are incorporated into each PDM activity box. In this example, dates are expressed in terms of the number of days after project start-up. Once the start date is known, these are ordinarily converted to specific calendar dates.

The question of whether a particular activity is on the critical path can be answered by comparing the early dates and the late dates. For example, in Figure 9-14, the difference between the early start and late start of Activity C is six days. This means that Activity C could start any time during those six days without impacting the overall project schedule. However, notice the difference between the early start and late start of Activity B: zero. This means that Activity B has no flexibility (float) with regard to when it can start. Activity B is on the critical path.

The management implications of knowing which activities are on the critical path are obvious. These are the activities that you will pay the most attention to as you attempt to keep the project on schedule, because one day of slippage of a critical path activity would mean one day of slippage in the whole project.

> ### BEWARE OF THE "NEARLY CRITICAL"
>
> **TRICKS OF THE TRADE**
>
> Naturally you must pay close attention to critical path activities. However, watch out for activities that are almost on the critical path—those with just a handful of float days. Pay even more attention if these nearly critical activities are difficult, uncertain, or risky. If you don't pay attention to the nearly critical activities, they may surprise you—and not in a good way!

One final note about critical path. Remember our discussion of the importance of keeping your schedule up to date throughout the life of the project? One good reason for that ties to the critical path concept. The critical path is also a "living" entity. In other words, as activities are completed ahead of schedule or behind schedule, the critical path changes. If you don't recognize a change in the critical path through your ongoing schedule updates, you could easily reach a point where you are spending time, money, and resources fighting fires that don't necessarily matter (i.e., not on the critical path) and not addressing your actual problem areas!

Identifying How Much You'll Spend (Cost Management)

The third dimension of the project plan is its cost. Cost management, however, is more than calculating the cost of the overall project. Cost management also consists of creating a budget (identifying the cost of individual work elements) and charting when the money will be spent. Let's begin with some basic definitions.

Types of Costs

Properly estimating and budgeting project funds aren't always easy as there are so many types of project expenditures. Here are some of the kinds of project costs you will need to consider:

- **Internal labor:** The cost of the people who work at your company assigned to execute project activities. This is often the largest component of a project budget.
- **External labor:** The cost of the people from outside your company who work on your project; often referred to as *contract* (or *subcontract*) *labor.*
- **Purchased materials:** The cost of raw materials, such as metal, wood, plastic, etc.; ordinarily purchased from vendors or suppliers.
- **Purchased hardware or software:** The cost of these items is often integrated into final project deliverables.
- **Purchased or leased supplies and equipment:** The cost of items consumed by the project and used in the process of executing it, for example, buying office supplies or renting a crane.
- **Purchased facilities:** This would be included only if the facilities are built or purchased solely for use in the project (in other words, when it's part of what the project delivers).
- **Leased facilities:** Rental space used in the process of executing the project (temporary office space, for example).
- **Training:** Training specifically required to achieve project success. This cost is often associated with customer-related training during installation or start-up.
- **Travel and other miscellaneous costs:** Again, the only rule here is that the expenditure must be required to execute the project.

If your project uses internal labor, become familiar with how your company addresses the practice of applying *fully burdened chargeout rates*. This is an hourly labor rate that your company's finance personnel will know (and should publish). It includes overhead—an amount above and beyond salaries (typically 30–50 percent) to make allowances for the indirect costs that the company must incur to conduct business. In some companies, this will be a flat rate for all project resources, and in other companies it might vary, depending on the nature of the skill set (e.g., engineering versus IT versus maintenance). To determine how much that resource will cost you on the project, multiply the fully burdened chargeout rate(s) times the number of hours that an internal resource will be working on your project (his or her effort).

Using the WBS for Cost Management

Remember our discussion on nifty uses for the WBS? Well, here are two more. You can use the WBS as both an estimating worksheet and as your primary structure for displaying the cost allocations to project activities. Both can be accomplished by using the format illustrated in Figure 9-15. Here, a WBS has been adapted to create a fill-in-the-blank worksheet for estimating costs. When completed, it automatically displays the project cost allocations.

The example shown in Figure 9-15 could be published using only the information under the heading "WBS Activities with Costs" (WBS Level 3), or it could be expanded to include the added detail shown in the entire chart. You'll have to use your judgment to determine whether this is the amount of detail desired by your management or stakeholders.

WBS Activities with Cost Subtotals			Internal Labor	Material	Contract Labor	Equipment Rent/Lease	Facility Rent/Lease
Project **XYZ** $785,000	10X-Design $70,900	101-Mechanical $18,700	$18,700	$1,000	$0	$1,200	$0
		102-Electrical $19,900	$19,900	$1,400	$0	$800	$0
		103-Software $32,200	$32,300	$2,200	$3,400	$300	$32,400

Figure 9-15. Using the WBS for cost estimating

What About Project Management Software?

We've placed this topic at the end of this chapter for a reason. Unfortunately, some people view project scheduling software as the totality of project management. This is an unhealthy perspective. While there's little doubt that scheduling software can be valuable, an inordinate focus on it belies the huge breadth of project management practices. As stated previously, project planning is more than a schedule, and project management is more than manipulating software.

LEARN THE BASICS FIRST!
CAUTION Take the time to fully understand the basics of project management before worrying about project management software. If you don't do this, you could end up in trouble. Remember: Using project management software is not the same as doing project management. Software is simply the automation of project management. A client once told us a funny (but true) adage: "Using scheduling software without understanding project management merely enables someone to create bad schedules—faster."

Excessive reliance on the tool discounts the importance of the "art" part of the project management discussed at the beginning of this book. Managing people is widely viewed as being crucial to project success. However, some software companies actually advertise that their tool "allows team members to send project status updates to the project manager electronically, thereby eliminating the need to get together." This is touted as if meeting with your team is a wasteful thing. With the obvious exception of virtual teams, this is an appalling feature to promote as a benefit to project managers.

Selecting the Right Project Management Software

People often ask, "What's the best project management software?" By now, you should know the standard answer in project management is ... It depends. In this case, it depends on many factors. Here are some of the factors you should consider as you select the right project management software for you:

Cost Versus functionality. The costs and capabilities of project management software vary. Systems can cost anywhere from a few hundred dollars to tens of thousands of dollars. Consider how much power you need with respect to the size of the project that the software can handle and the features you're likely to need or benefit from. Keep an eye on the future: consider functionality not only in terms of what you need now, but for the near term as well.

Capability versus ease of use. The capability of project management software tends to be proportional to the difficulty in using it. We knew of a company whose need for computing power in their project management software was not great. However, the decision makers felt they wanted maximum horsepower—just in case. Unfortunately, using this high-powered tool required them to send people to a monthlong, intensive training program and to periodic refresher courses thereafter. The company had difficulty breaking people free to take the training, not to mention the expense. After two years of hacking their way through the tool, they abandoned it and bought something simpler.

Compatibility with other systems. Consider how your project management software will have to interface with other communication, accounting, or reporting systems already in use in your company.

Documentation, start-up support, and ongoing technical support. How much support can you expect from the manufacturer and/or the company selling the software? Consider important issues such as the documentation you'll receive, the setup and start-up support you can expect, and the long-term technical support you'll get.

Go to several sources for input, including the experiences of others and rating guides, before selecting your project management software.

Words to the Wise About Project Management Software

The tremendous power of project management software can lull you into a false sense of security. Although the tool can save you a significant amount of time, recognize that there are many things it cannot do. For most project situations you'll face, you'll need to rely on your knowledge of project management rather than a software tool. Here are some things that the tool cannot do:

- **Make decisions.** You will still have to determine the course of the project through the day-to-day decisions you make.

■ **Gather data.** You must still determine how much data you need and what forms are most useful to manage your project.

■ **Find errors.** If you input bad data, you will receive bad data.

■ **Solve your most critical problems.** Some of the biggest problems you'll encounter relate to people. Obviously, project management software can't address this issue.

■ **Manage people (and people issues).** Only you can do that!

Key Documentation Used to Develop an Integrated Project Plan

At this stage of the project implementation life cycle, the scope of work is identified through a Work Breakdown Structure. Then you develop a schedule using network diagramming techniques (which model the optimum sequence of activities) and estimated activity durations to create a Project Control Schedule (which defines when resources will be applied). Use a worksheet approach (using the WBS as a template) to estimate the cost of the project—and the cost of individual activities. From these estimates, you can create a cash flow model showing the rate at which monies will be spent. Finally, develop a budget to help yourself manage the project costs. These steps converge through the creation of a baseline Integrated Project Plan.

Let's review these planning documents—all of which are illustrated in Figure 9-16.

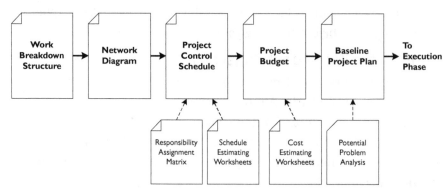

Figure 9-16. Key documents in the project planning process

Work Breakdown Structure. The Work Breakdown Structure (WBS) is perhaps the most foundational planning document; just about every other planning document is an extension of the WBS. The WBS lists and organizes into logical subgroups all the work (activities) required to execute the project.

Network Diagram. Also called *logic diagram*, the Network Diagram depicts the sequence of the activities. It's the natural starting point for the scheduling process, and it's a critical document in schedule development.

Project Control Schedule (Gantt Chart). The Project Control Schedule is a time-scaled bar chart. It uses the logic developed in the Network Diagram, considers the length of time it takes to execute individual activities, factors in resource availability, and places everything into calendar time. It's the document of choice for helping the team focus on what needs to be done and when. A Project Control Schedule is used primarily as an internal control document for the project team and some stakeholders. Progress evaluation, variance calculation, and continuous forecasting are all done using the Project Control Schedule.

Responsibility Assignment Matrix. The Responsibility Assignment Matrix (RAM) is a two-axis chart that shows how work is assigned. It correlates specific work elements with specific task performers.

Schedule Estimating Worksheets. Schedule Estimating Worksheets are directly related to the basis of estimate concept mentioned several times throughout this book. A basis of estimate describes the assumptions and procedures used in arriving at any and all estimates you receive from estimators. Schedule Estimating Worksheets should include the assumptions, calculations, and other information used to estimate required labor hours and the activity durations you would use to create your Project Control Schedule. Request a copy of these worksheets, place them in your project files, and refer to them whenever you encounter change.

Project Budget (Cost Estimates). You should prepare a budget for each project. Provide estimates for each activity and for the total project. These estimates become the basis for cost tracking and control.

Cost Estimating Worksheets. Just like Schedule Estimating Worksheets, Cost Estimating Worksheets are also related to the concept of basis of estimate. As the title suggests, Cost Estimating Worksheets would include the assumptions, calculations, and other information used to estimate the expenditure required to execute each activity included in your overall project budget. Request a copy of these worksheets, place them in your project files, and refer to them whenever you encounter change.

Baseline Project Plan. The Baseline Project Plan includes all the other documents shown in Figure 9-16. In this figure, the Baseline Project Plan appears to lead directly to execution. Although this is true from a document flow perspective, the reality is that many organizations require formal management approval before proceeding to project execution. This formal approval is what constitutes the notion of a "baseline." Referring to this edition as the Baseline Plan signifies that this is the plan that everyone will work from, and that this is the plan against which you will measure project variances.

Potential Problem Analysis. Potential Problem Analysis (PPA) is a risk management technique to identify what may go wrong on your project, so that you can take steps to compensate. This technique is described in the next chapter. Although a PPA can be performed at any time, an excellent time is immediately after creating the project plan. The PPA process normally generates a considerable amount of documentation. Keep copies of these documents in your project files.

Manager's Checklist for Chapter 9

☑ Develop a Project Management Configuration Plan (PMCP) at the start of every project you manage. This plan describes how you intend to implement project management methods on your project.

☑ The term scope has two meanings: *project scope* refers to the high-level objectives of the project; *scope of work* collectively refers to the activities to be performed. The first step in developing an Integrated Project Plan is identifying and breaking down the work to be done. The Work Breakdown Structure (WBS) is the preferred tool for doing this.

☑ Work Breakdown Structures can be adapted to serve many planning functions, such as an estimating worksheet.

☑ Preparing a Network Diagram with your entire team using sticky notes is an efficient technique—and an excellent team-building exercise.

☑ The "size" of an activity can be characterized in two ways: *effort* refers to how many labor hours will be logged to the activity (used for *cost* management); *duration* refers to the window of time within which the activity will be started and completed (used for *schedule* management). You'll need to track both.

☑ The critical path is the longest path through the schedule. There is no margin for error with respect to when these activities in the critical path can be done. By definition, delaying a critical path activity means delaying the project.

☑ There are many types of costs. Make sure you've accounted for all of them in your cost estimate.

☑ Don't fall into the trap of believing that project management software will manage your project for you. It's only a tool.

Addressing Risk and Uncertainty

B rad pours himself a cup of coffee as he surveys the break room. He's looking for someone he can brag to about the great job he and his team have done in putting together a solid project plan. He spots Ted, a veteran project manager, and sits down across the table from him. After a few minutes of discussion about the weather, Ted provides the opening that Brad is looking for.

"So, Brad," says Ted, "How's it going on Project Apex? That's a pretty hot project. I hope you've got everything under control."

"You bet," says Brad as he grins from ear to ear. "The planning took a little longer than I expected, but we've definitely got everything under control."

Brad continues by describing some of the details of Project Apex. Ted listens intently as Brad weaves a tale of an intricately crafted schedule, the key project players he's been able to recruit, the hard bargains he drove with suppliers, and the well-timed arrangement he worked out with the client for shutting down specific production lines just when Brad's team needs them.

"Yes, sir," Brad concludes, "We've got everything nailed down, and we're ready to go!" Then he adds, "So what do you think, Ted? Not bad for my first time out the chute, eh?"

Brad leans back and awaits affirmation from his experienced colleague.

Ted ponders for a moment, then poses this question:

"What happens if Jason gets taken off your project? You know how they're always sending him off to the latest trouble spot."

Brad's grin begins to fade.

"And what are you going to do if Accutrex doesn't deliver your parts on time? You've got a backup plan, right?"

"Uhh, right," says Brad, as his grin fades.

"And what happens if the demand shifts and the client won't let you in to work on the production lines at some later time? That could create a significant schedule problem if your resources aren't available then. You've told management that's a possibility, haven't you?"

"Well, not in so many words," Brad says, as he excuses himself from the table.

As Brad walks back to his desk, he begins to understand what's happened. In his enthusiasm, optimism, and desire to display a can-do attitude, he hasn't given enough thought to everything that could go wrong on Project Apex—and what he could do about it.

"Projects are risky business," Brad thinks to himself as he contemplates his next move. He waits a few minutes—just long enough for Ted to get back to his office—then picks up the phone. Ted has raised some good questions; maybe he can help Brad come up with some answers.

Overview of Risk and Uncertainty

Have you ever seen the toy cars that go fast in a particular direction, only to bump into a solid structure and change direction? They continue to bump into things and change direction until they eventually run out of energy.

If you attempt to manage a project without addressing risk and uncertainty, you'll soon begin to feel much like one of those toys. You will continually bump into things that will throw you in an unplanned direction. And before long, you'll abandon your original project plan (the one you and your team spent so much time developing) and begin to live by an uncomfortable combination of your wits and the seat of your pants.

Risk and uncertainty are unavoidable in project life, and it's dangerous to ignore or deny their impact. Adopting a can-do attitude may be a good way to get your team members energized and committed, but it's a reckless approach when it comes to managing a complex project.

Some Basic Definitions

Let's look at some of the key terms associated with risk management:

Uncertainty: Are you surprised that I didn't start with the definition of *risk*? That's because uncertainty actually drives every aspect of risk management. We define *uncertainty* as an absence of information, knowledge, or understanding regarding a situation, condition, action, decision, or event. Project managers constantly suffer from an absence of information, knowledge, or understanding.

Risk: In our daily lives, we tend to think of risk as something bad that could happen to us. But in the world of project management, *risk* refers to your ability to predict a particular outcome with precision and certainty. It's a reflection of the amount of uncertainty that exists in a particular situation and is proportional to the amount of information you possess, as Figure 10-1 illustrates. This interpretation is derived from a study of decision and risk analysis, the statistical foundation of project risk management.

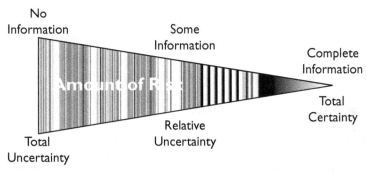

Figure 10-1. Relationship among information, uncertainty, and risk

Threat: Threats ordinarily refer to the negative—or downside—effects of risk. *Threats* are specific events that drive your project in the direction of outcomes that are viewed as unfavorable (e.g., schedule delays, cost overruns, and inferior product performance). Risk (and uncertainty) can also

SMART

MANAGING

FOCUS ON THREATS

While the positive component of risk management—seizing opportunities—is certainly worthy of consideration, your time is generally best spent focusing on reducing or eliminating threats. Any time you can effectively counteract a threat, you reduce your chances of disappointing key stakeholders by not fulfilling their expectations. Also, experience suggests that you are likely to encounter more factors that can make things bad for you than factors that can make things better.

refer to positive things as well. The positive effects of risk are called *opportunities*.

Managing Risk: An Overview

A variety of specific methods exist that prescribe how you can deal with risk and the threats (or opportunities) it produces. Most of these methods follow some variation of the same four steps. Before discussing the steps, I'd like to briefly describe these steps, focusing on the downside (threats).

Step 1. Identification: Determine potential problems. Identify all significant uncertainties related to your project (areas where you have limited control or information on something that can impact your ability to deliver as promised). Express them as specific threats (potential problems).

Step 2. Quantification: Determine the size and nature of potential problems. Obtain data, insights, and estimates on the range of possible outcomes for all uncertainties and potential problems. This should include distribution and/or probabilities of occurrence throughout that range, so as to better understand the nature of the threats and their potential effects on the project.

KEY TERM

Risk assessment The combination of risk identification, risk quantification, and risk analysis. The primary output of a thorough risk assessment is a list of specific, well-defined potential problems (threats) and a determination of which could have the greatest impact on your ability to deliver your predicted (or promised) project outcomes.

Step 3. Analysis: Determine the high-threat problems. Use the knowledge gained in steps 1 and 2 to evaluate which potential problems represent the greatest dangers to achieving a successful and predictable project outcome. This is typically accomplished by considering two key attributes of each threat: the likelihood that it will occur (called *probability*) and its anticipated effect on the project, if it were to occur (called *impact*).

Step 4. Response: Deal with the high-threat problems. Determine the best way to deal with the each high-threat potential problem, which may include evaluating and choosing among a number of alternatives and creating specific action plans.

Now let's take a closer look at each of these four steps.

Step 1. Identify What Can Hurt You (Risk Identification)

The first step in the risk management process is figuring out what you're up against. What types of issues could threaten your ability to deliver what you've promised? As mentioned earlier, it all begins with the uncertainty of not knowing exactly how things are going to turn out. This is another way of saying that many aspects of projects are unpredictable despite our best efforts to nail them down. Figure 10-2 lists some of the most common areas of uncertainty that exist on many projects.

Problems can develop from these sources of uncertainty. Problems are what you need to uncover. Specific potential problems. As many as you can think of. But how do you go about identifying problems? There's no magic formula for identifying potential threats to your project. It's going to require specific knowledge of the project, significant brainpower, and the ability to speculate. Hmm . . . that sounds like an excellent opportunity for a team-building event.

In Chapter 7, we discussed how some of the best team-building events are those where team members expand their knowledge of each other and the project at the same time. Identifying potential problems as a team is an ideal way to accomplish that. Begin by getting the entire team together for two to four hours, depending on project size and complexity. Gather every piece of documentation you can and urge others to do the same. Typical background documents may include the Business Case, the Client Require-

Area	Description
Scope	Estimated extent of the work, ability to clearly define work, design errors and omissions, customer-driven scope change
Time	Estimated project duration, estimated activity duration, time-to-market, launch date, timing of management reviews and approvals
Cost	Estimated project costs, downstream manufacturing costs, downstream maintenance costs, inflation, currency exchange, budget limitation
Technology	Customer expectations, probability of success, ability to scale-up, product manufacturability, design success
Resources	Quantity, quality, availability, skill match, ability to define roles and responsibilities
Organizational	Client's priorities and knowledge, coordination among departments
Marketability	User expectations, sales volume, pricing, share, demographics, quality, geography, economy
Outside factors	Competitor actions or reactions, regulations

Figure 10-2. Typical areas of high uncertainty on projects

ments Document, and the Project Definition Document. Of more immediate value will be your project planning documents, such as the WBS, the Integrated Project Plan (Control Schedule), and the Responsibility Assignment Matrix. Finally, assemble all relevant support documents, such as basis of estimate sheets, planning assumptions, and network diagrams used to create the Control Schedule. It's helpful to have as many documents as possible on hand to stimulate thinking about potential problems. A checklist of specific potential problems can also be helpful. Figure 10-3 lists more than 60 common problems encountered on projects.

List as many potential problems as you can, using brainstorming techniques. Although you don't want to stifle creativity, pare the list to a reasonable size (perhaps 30 to 50, depending on project size and complexity).

As you list potential problems that could threaten your project, don't lose sight of the concept of uncertainty. Remember that the lack of infor-

Project Scope	Facilities and Equipment	Personal
__ Client adds scope or features	__ Lack of availability	__ Vacations/illnesses
__ Work cannot be accurately defined	__ Poor reliability	__ Family/other issues
__ Scope is underestimated	__ Incompatibility w/ existing	__ Conflicting interests
__ Project objectives change	__ Competing uses or users	__ Outside distractions
Project Schedule	__ Proprietary limitations	__ Ethics issues
__ Project duration underestimated	__ Poor flexibility/adaptability	__ Moral issues
__ End date shifts during project	__ Undesirable location	**People/Interpersonal**
__ End date is unrealistic	__ Space (lack of, wrong type)	__ Performance/productivity
__ Project approvals are late	**Resources**	__ Interpersonal conflict
__ Management reviews delay project	__ Team members change	__ Development and growth
Marketing	__ Funding shifts or freezes	__ Poor motivation and attitudes
__ Unrealistic user expectations	__ Uncertain costs/expenses	__ Poor skills fit
__ Market requirements shift	__ Unavailability of resources	__ Health and safety issues
__ Price point changes	__ Misaligned priorities	__ Diversity issues
__ Sales volume goes down	**Organizational**	**External Influences**
__ Sales volume goes up	__ Unclear roles/responsibilities	__ Weather, natural disasters
Material	__ Poor delegation	__ Government regulations
__ Source(s) and availability	__ Poor relationships among units	__ Health/Safety/OSHA
__ Poor integration w/ existing	__ Lack of proper coordination	__ Patent, copyright issues
__ Poor supplier reliability	__ Potential turf wars	__ Cultural barriers
__ Poor material reliability	__ Policy limitations	__ Political tensions
__ Substandard quality	__ Poor communications	__ Economic trend shifts
__ High price	__ Line versus staff issues	__ Poor company image
	__ Reorganization issues	__ Unfavorable legal position

Figure 10-3. Checklist of specific potential problems

CONSIDER COMBINATIONS OF PROBLEMS

TRICKS OF THE TRADE

Many people who think about potential problems have a tendency to think in just one dimension—that is, one potential problem occurring in isolation. Encourage everyone whom you ask to brainstorm about potential problems to also think of combinations of problems. Two specific problems may not represent much of a threat when considered independently, but together they may spell disaster. Also, when considered together, two problems may characterize a cause-and-effect relationship that needs to be addressed. An excellent example of this surfaced at the beginning of the chapter when Ted asked Brad, "What if the client won't let you in to work on the production lines at some later time? That could create a significant schedule problem if your resources aren't available then."

mation, knowledge, and understanding is really your enemy. Anything you can do to acquire useful information—in a cost-effective way—is probably a good investment.

Step 2. Assess the Potential Damage (Risk Quantification)

OK, you've listed a number of things that could go wrong. But how big is the threat that each one poses? You need to quantify the magnitude of what you're up against. Do this by gathering insights into the potential problems you've identified in step 1. For each problem, characterize and quantify these two basic characteristics:

1. Nature or extent of the problem. Let's say that a labor strike is possible, which would impact the availability of some contracted resources. Which work groups would be involved? What specific resources could become unavailable? Would other work groups be affected, even though they're not in the striking group? When might this happen? Would this impact the project timeline? If so, by how much? How much would it affect the project budget? Do I have options for working around the striking groups, perhaps through other resources? Would using other resources impact the quality of some deliverables?

2. Nature or extent of the effect. Let's say that the same strike could cause a schedule delay. How much of a delay? A week? Two weeks? A month? Will the project necessarily be delayed by that same amount?

Many more issues and questions could be related to this problem. To get the full picture about the nature and extent of problems and their effects, you will have to rely on a variety of sources, such as:

- Survey data (preference, opinion, etc.)
- Historical data
- Product specification sheets
- Mock-ups, simulations, or pilot studies
- Research and tests
- Subject matter experts' (SME) opinion and judgment

In making your final determinations, weigh the knowledge and credibility of your sources—particularly if you receive conflicting information. You have to decide whether to use information that is conservative or cautious, or use averages.

Step 3. Determine the Biggest Threats to Your Project (Risk Analysis)

At this point, you and your team have identified a substantial list of potential problems. You've tried to quantify the extent of these problems and their potential effects on your project. You quickly realize that you don't have the resources to deal with every one of these potential problems. So how do you reduce the list to a manageable size? How do you identify the problems that threaten you the most and, therefore, demand your attention?

One of the most common and straightforward methods consists of making subjective judgments about two critical attributes of potential problems—probability and impact. These terms mean exactly what you would expect. *Probability* is the likelihood that the potential problem will occur. *Impact* is the seriousness or severity of the potential problem in terms of its effect on your project.

DEFINE WHAT YOU MEAN BY IMPACT

When assessing the probability and impact of potential problems, a 5- or 10-point rating scale is often used. Whatever scale you choose, take time to clarify the terms you use. Probability, although subjective in nature, is generally clear. People readily understand the concept of percentages. However, defining how a potential problem may impact a project can be confusing unless you use specific, descriptive terminology. For example, would a four-week schedule delay be considered minor? serious? catastrophic? As we have often observed … It depends. By using good descriptors, everyone will have a sense of what any given impact score really means. Without this type of clarification, differences in understanding could further undermine a process that is already subjective.

Once the probability and impact have been identified, it's easy to determine the high-threat problems—those that yield the largest number when you multiply probability and impact. (For simplicity, let's call this the *threat rating.*) Figure 10-4 offers a graphical representation of this concept.

Responding to some high-threat problems could consume a considerable amount of resources, so you must be prudent in deciding how many you choose to take further action on. Establish the maximum num-

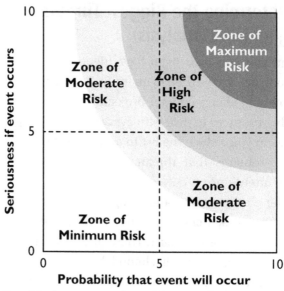

Figure 10-4. Graphical representation of threat ratings

ber of problems you will address and/or a predetermined minimum threat rating. If you use a 5-point scoring scale, a threat rating of around 10 is probably a reasonable lower limit. Use the threat rating to prioritize the problems you intend to address.

Step 4. Address the High-Threat Problems (Risk Response)

Several options exist with regard to how you will address the high-threat problems. Let's examine these options for dealing with risk and potential problems:

Avoidance: Avoidance does not mean that you ignore a problem or threat. It means you choose a course of action whereby you are no longer exposed to the threat. This often means you're now pursuing a completely different course from the one you had originally planned. The launch of a telecommunications satellite provides an example of this. Launches are carefully planned, but may be postponed if poor weather conditions should arise. In choosing to delay the launch, the problem of poor weather is avoided.

Transfer: In transfer, you shift the consequence of the threat. A common example of risk transfer is something we're all familiar with—insurance. Risk transfer does not address the actual risk—it makes another party responsible for the impact of the risk.

Prevention: Prevention refers to actions taken to reduce the probability of occurrence of a problem. Ordinarily, it will be your first course of action in dealing with high-threat problems. Prevention begins by identifying the root causes of potential problems. Determining root cause may allow you to identify preventive measures that could reduce the probability that a given problem will occur. Be sure to revise the project plan to incorporate any preventive actions that you intend to take so that they're not overlooked or forgotten.

Mitigation of impact: This strategy aims to reduce the negative effects of a potential problem. For example, installing air bags in automobiles does nothing to reduce the probability of accidents, but it may significantly reduce the effects. It's important to note that mitigation tactics may be viewed as a waste of time, money, and effort if the potential problem does not materialize, so you may want to apply these measures conservatively.

> ### AN OUNCE OF PREVENTION
>
> Prevention is generally the least costly and most reliable strategy for dealing with risk—particularly in situations where the impact is high. You should plan and execute preventive measures whenever you can.

Contingency planning: Contingency plans are specific actions that will be taken if—and only if—a potential problem occurs. Although intended to deal with problems only after they've occurred, contingency plans should be developed in advance. This helps ensure a coordinated, effective, and timely response. Also, some plans may require backup resources that need to be arranged for in advance. Contingency planning should be done only for the high-threat problems that remain after you've taken preventive measures.

Assumption: Assumption means you are aware of the risk, but choose to take no action on it. You're agreeing to accept its consequences or to sim-

SMART MANAGING

BUILD WARNING MECHANISMS

Whenever you formulate a contingency plan, be sure to identify a specific condition, event, or threshold that could trigger a problem, alerting the project team that it's time to put the contingency plan into effect. It's advisable to incorporate the trigger into the project plan.

ply deal with them if the problem happens. That's essentially how you're treating threats that fall below the threat threshold described above. Assumption is also a valid strategy in situations where the consequences of the threat are less costly and/or less traumatic than the effort required to prevent them.

Managing Project Risk Is a Mindset

The process above describes a step-by-step method for reviewing and analyzing your project. However, risk management is not only a process—it's a mindset that requires your ongoing attention. From the start of your project, risk and uncertainty will be ever-present threats.

Even though you may feel that you've effectively dealt with risk by using a process such as the one outlined above, some amount of ongoing maintenance will be required. The size and shape of threats continually change, so you must monitor them on an ongoing basis. Be attentive to any preventive measures to make sure they're addressing the threats as intended. You must remain vigilant for triggers—the points that alert you to the need to pursue a contingency plan. And always be on the lookout for the existence of new threats. New threats will not necessarily be obvious. In short, you should always be looking for trouble. Be skeptical, aggressive, and relentless in your quest to uncover potential problems. As the saying goes, if you don't manage risk, it will manage you.

You Can't Fix Everything: Learn to Accommodate Uncertainty

Potential problems are specific manifestations of the uncertainty that exists in all projects. Properly dealing with specific threats reduces the downside variability of the final project outcome. In common terms, it is intended to protect your project from harmful events.

However, despite your best efforts to identify and address threats, a large number of circumstances (think of them as little threats) will remain that you won't be able to identify or have the resources to address. In addition, many things can happen that you cannot foresee or predict. That's why variability should be viewed as an inescapable project reality.

You cannot make the inherent variability in projects go away. Consequently, you must acknowledge and accommodate it. Recognize, evaluate, estimate, and communicate its existence to your management and other stakeholders as appropriate. Following are some strategies you can use to accomplish this.

Use Ranged Values When Expressing Estimated Outcomes

This is a strong recommendation that we routinely make to all project managers. From now on, whenever you are asked to provide an estimate for anything, express the estimate as a range of possible outcomes, rather than a specific value. The reason behind this is simple: any estimate has two dimensions. The first dimension is the raw number itself, for example, an estimated expenditure of $110,000. The second dimension is the level of certainty around the raw number.

If you had excellent insight and information about the previous estimate, you might say, "We expect the cost to be between $105,000 and $115,000.

But what if a great deal of uncertainty existed? In that case you should say, "We expect the cost to be somewhere between $90,000 and $140,000." These two statements express very different sentiments about uncertainty—and that's a good thing. In fact, one of the worst things you can do with regard to estimating is to create an illusion of accuracy through precision.

Here's an example: Let's say that a project manager predicts the cost of a large work package will be $112,370—because that's the value that his or her calculation produced. Without any qualifying remarks (namely, a range around that estimate), this will probably be interpreted as an estimate having a high degree of certainty. Often, that is not the case, due to the inherent uncertainty in all project work. The result may be a large and unpleasant misunderstanding when that work package actually costs $126,000. When providing the original estimate, the project manager knew that circumstances suggested this higher outcome was possible, but never communicated this to others.

Use Three-Point Estimates

A technique called *three-point estimating* can be used in conjunction with any estimated value. This technique recognizes the variability innate in everything, and applies rudimentary statistics in a way that accommodates and expresses that variability. In project scheduling, for example, we discussed the need to estimate activity durations. For many years, the Program Evaluation and Review Technique (PERT) approach was used to establish a sound, risk-based estimate of duration for activities placed in a schedule. While PERT has been superseded by the Monte Carlo approach that's built into today's estimating software, PERT nonetheless offers an excellent study in the practice of three-point estimating. The PERT calculation calls for three estimates to be provided for each activity:

1. **Pessimistic duration:** The duration if things go poorly
2. **Optimistic duration:** The duration if things go smoothly
3. **Most likely duration:** Your best guess

Figure 10-5 offers more insight into this technique for accommodating uncertainty.

The formula often used in conjunction with the PERT estimating method (although it could be used at any time) is as follows:

$$\frac{O+4M+P}{6} \quad \text{where} \quad \begin{array}{l} O = \text{the } \textbf{optimistic} \text{ estimate of task duration} \\ M = \text{the } \textbf{most likely} \text{ estimate of task duration} \\ P = \text{the } \textbf{pessimistic} \text{ estimate of task duration} \end{array}$$

Statistically, this formula "favors" the most likely, but allows for some adjustment to accommodate extremes in minimum or maximum outcome.

Sample Calculations

Optimistic	Most Likely	Pessimistic	Risk-Adjusted Duration
5	7	15	8
8	17	20	16
16	17	30	19

Figure 10-5. The PERT technique for three-point estimating

> **PERT** (a useful history lesson) PERT is an acronym for Program Evaluation and Review Technique, a method used in project management for years. Many people erroneously refer to the network diagrams with lines and bubbles as *PERT charts*. **KEY TERM** They think the bubbles are what makes that particular network diagram a PERT chart. What really characterizes PERT is the use of a probabilistic approach. PERT uses three-point estimating and basic arithmetic to determine risk-adjusted activity durations. It can also be used to calculate the probabilities of specific project outcomes when used in what-if studies.

Using Commercially Available Estimating Software

Estimating software is useful in helping people understand the process of estimating under uncertainty. Many products are available that use the power of statistics to create probabilistic estimates. These software tools are powerful, yet easy to use—and inexpensive. Most function the same way, following the approach described below. (This is an example of cost estimating; the procedure for estimating a schedule is more complex, but similar in approach.)

Step 1. Calculate minimum, maximum, and most likely estimates. That's the three-point estimating technique we discussed earlier. While the principle is similar, the software tool takes the evaluation to a much greater depth. Figure 10-6 shows a portion of a typical input form.

Step 2. Select the appropriate risk profile. The *risk profile* describes the distribution of potential costs for each activity across the entire range of values for that activity (between the minimum and maximum costs). For example, Profile A in Figure 10-7 suggests that the cost of the activity would be just as likely to be one value as any other value in the range. A triangular distribution (Profile B) suggests that the greatest chance of the activity cost will be near the peak of the triangle. The triangular distribution is often used, as it a reasonable assumption, and does not require the user to input anything beyond the minimum, maximum, and most likely values. Entering data for this profile consists of nothing more than a simple push of a button.

Step 3. Incorporate dependencies into the model. In this step, you define any dependent (if-then) relationships that may exist between activities. Dependencies are not common in cost estimating, but are important

Task Name	Minimum Cost	Most Likely Cost	Maximum Cost	Risk Profile
1.3 Purchase Materials				
1.3.1 Equipment	$190,000	$200,000	$280,000	A
1.3.2 Electrical	$18,000	$20,000	$24,000	A
1.3.3 Process Control	$27,000	$30,000	$39,000	A
1.4 Installation				
1.4.1 Site Prep	$9,500	$10,000	$20,000	C
1.4.2 Concrete	$22,500	$25,000	$37,500	B
1.4.3 Steel	$27,000	$30,000	$39,000	B
1.4.4 Buildings	$22,500	$25,000	$31,300	D
1.4.5 Equipment	$81,000	$90,000	$126,000	D
1.4.6 Piping	$99,000	$110,000	$137,500	A
1.4.7 Electrical	$81,000	$90,000	$117,000	A
1.4.8 Process Control	$90,000	$100,000	$130,000	B
1.4.9 Coatings	$9,000	$10,000	$12,000	C
1.4.10 Other	$9,000	$10,000	$15,000	C
Total		$750,000		

Figure 10-6. Input form for statistical estimating software

when operating in the scheduling realm, where the sequence of activities is important.

Step 4. Run the simulation. At this point the statistical software uses your inputs to simulate the execution of your project as many times as you wish—usually 500 to 1,000 times.

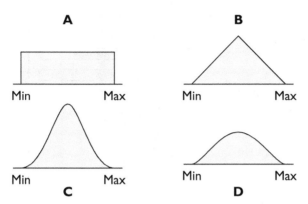

Figure 10-7. Common risk profiles

Step 5. Evaluate and interpret the results. Figure 10-8 illustrates the various outputs that are available.

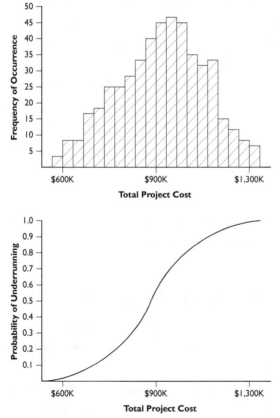

Figure 10-8. Top (a) Frequency distribution chart; bottom (b) Probability curve (continued on next page)

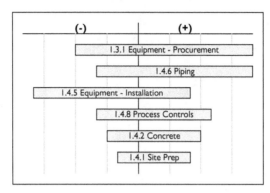

Figure 10-8. (c) Tornado diagram (continued)

Figure 10-8(a) is called a *frequency distribution chart*. It shows how many times your project would be completed at a particular cost. Note the characteristic shape of a normal distribution; this is fairly common.

Figure 10-8(b) is a *probability curve*. This chart offers the greatest opportunity to illustrate important points when making proposals or presentations. For example, this chart reveals that there's a 20 percent chance that the project would cost less than $800,000, a 50 percent chance that the project will exceed $900,000, and a 10 percent chance that the final expenditure would exceed $1.2 million. Displaying estimating data like this reinforces the argument that using point estimates does not tell a complete story. Finally, Figure 10-8(c) is called a *tornado diagram*, based on its obvious resemblance to one. This chart illustrates which activities have the largest potential to impact the final project cost.

Together, these graphical outputs—and the use of estimating software such as this—educates people on the uncertainty and inherent variability in all projects.

Manager's Checklist for Chapter 10

☑ Don't let a can-do attitude inhibit your ability to understand that bad things can happen to your project. If you don't manage risk, it will manage you.

☑ In the world of project management, risk is directly related to uncertainty and the extent to which you can predict a specific outcome or understand the nature of a given situation.

☑ The focus of your risk management efforts should be on addressing the downside effects of risk or threats.

☑ There are four basic steps in managing downside risk: (1) identify what threats may exist, (2) quantify those threats, (3) determine which threats require further action, and (4) take action either to reduce the probability that the threat will occur or to lessen its effects if it does.

☑ Perform risk management analyses with your entire team. It represents an excellent team-building opportunity.

☑ Not all risk can be eliminated. Sometimes you must acknowledge or accommodate its existence. A good example of this is providing estimates that use ranges of values rather than specific numbers.

☑ Strongly consider the use of commercially available software for cost and schedule estimating. It's a powerful, easy-to-use tool.

Ensuring Successful Project Execution

W e are nearly at the end of the book and are just now getting to the subject of project execution. There's a lesson in that. The time you spend laying the foundation of a project—in the form of justification, requirements gathering, definition, team building, project planning, and risk assessment—is likely to be a fraction of the time you would spend in a state of chaos, confusion, and rework if you had blindly jumped into the project.

Another important point must be made. Although we have spent a proportionately long time addressing these topics in this book, the proportions are different in real life. You will spend 5 to 10 times more in project execution than you will in establishing your project. If you do a high-quality job of laying a proper foundation, you will be rewarded by spending a great deal of time enjoying a sense of calmness and control during the execution phase.

Speaking of execution, Brad is now ready to execute Project Apex. He and his team have prepared a plan and examined the potential risks. Now it's time to get down to work. His biggest concern at this point is to keep Project Apex headed in the right direction. But as he considers the complexity of his project, questions begin to swirl in his head.

"Am I supposed to be telling everybody what to do all the time?"

"Should I just wait for problems to pop up?"

"What exactly am I supposed to be *controlling*?"

Once again, Brad feels overwhelmed.

Then he remembers his colleague, Ted, who helped Brad understand risk management. Brad picks up the phone and dials Ted's number.

What Project Control Really Means

The word *control* has several meanings. Some managers are initially dismayed by the use of that word, because they mistakenly equate it with notions of discipline and authority. In the world of project management, control has little to do with telling people what to do, dictating their actions or plans, or trying to force them to behave in a certain way—all of which are common interpretations of *control*.

In project management, *control* is analogous to steering a ship. It's about continually adjusting course with one objective in mind—bringing the ship into a safe harbor, as promised at the start of the voyage. The successful project/voyage includes identifying a specific destination, carefully charting a course to get there, evaluating your location throughout the voyage, and keeping a watchful eye on any challenges that lie in your course.

The Purpose of Project Control

Fledgling as well as some experienced project managers often make the same mistake when trying to control their projects: they get wrapped up in the here-and-now—the measurement and evaluation of their immediate situation—to the exclusion of all else. They calculate their current position and how far off course they are. That's what they report to management and promise to fix. Their entire focus consists of staying on the course they've drawn from the beginning to end of the project. Unfortunately, controlling your project's destiny is not that simple.

As we'll see, evaluating where you are vis-à-vis where you're supposed to be is certainly part of control, and getting back on course is almost always a sound strategy. But your primary mission is to deliver what you've promised, so you should think of maintaining control in terms of minimizing the distance between where you end up and where you said you'd end up.

This means that project control requires an eye on the future, as the following formulas show:

**Calculated Present Variance + Estimated Future Variance
= Final Project Variance**

or, in terms of project outcome:

**Current Performance (or Position) + Forecasted Future Performance
= Final Outcome**

These simple formulas can be applied to virtually any project parameter—cost, schedule, deliverable quality, deliverable functionality, economic return, etc. The decisions you make during project execution should always be made with the end point in mind. There are two reasons for this.

First, when the destination is your primary focus, your decisions are likely to be more effective and lasting. Guiding the ship must include more than steering it immediately back on course. You must recognize that there's an object up ahead that you're going to have to steer around or that the current has picked up, propelling you faster than expected. The end of the project will always be different than what you expected at the project start. Assumptions will be revised, operating conditions will change, and unexpected obstacles will appear in your path. Sometimes, actions you take now must compensate for future sources of variance as well as variances created though past performance.

The second reason you need to focus on the end point pertains to management reporting. Management will want to know where you think you're going to end up, as this is the information they need to run the business. Being able to report to management that you're two weeks behind schedule or $10,000 over budget right now may not be of great value to them. Reporting that you expect the project to be completed three weeks late or $15,000 over budget is more likely to be of value.

What Are You Actually Controlling?

At this point you're probably saying, "OK, so I should focus on the end point of the project, and I should try to minimize variances. But how is the end point defined? And what kind of variance are we talking about?" Two valid questions.

These questions take us back to the discussion in Chapter 2 about the dimensions of project success. The most fundamental measure of project success (defined as Level 1 in Chapter 2) pertains to meeting basic project targets. These are targets that you promised to meet at the beginning of the project, so these should be the targets that you control. It's as simple as that!

As you may recall, two of the targets evaluate resource consumption:

1. **Schedule:** Was the project completed on time? (How long did we take?)
2. **Cost:** Did the project come in at cost? (How much did we spend?)

The other two targets evaluate project deliverables:

3. **Functionality:** Do project deliverables have the expected capability? (Can they perform the expected functions?)
4. **Quality:** Do the deliverables perform as well as promised? (How well do they perform?)

For any project manager the ideal end point occurs when a project meets these four targets exactly as promised. Although "beating the targets" is often characterized as desirable, hitting the targets provides a level of predictability that most managers value.

Sometimes, however, controlling cost and schedule gets too much attention and deliverable performance is not as closely monitored as it should be. This is a major oversight, one that you should concentrate on avoiding. We examine ways to maintain control over all four of these success dimensions as we move ahead.

SMART

MANAGING

PAY ATTENTION TO DELIVERABLE PERFORMANCE

Meeting cost and schedule targets often receives an inordinate amount of a project manager's attention. But if the quality and functionality of the project deliverables slip (which can happen in the quest to meet cost and schedule targets), an inferior product may result in client dissatisfaction. As part of your project control efforts, continually verify that the standards of deliverable performance that you promised are being maintained. Over the years, we have found there is much truth in this adage "If it cost too much or took too long, they might forget. If it doesn't work—they will never forget!"

Required Process Elements

Detailed project plans are created to satisfy two objectives: first, to provide a map for the project team to follow during project execution and second, to provide you with an instrument you can use to evaluate whether the project is staying on course. Simply stated, you won't be able to maintain control over the project if you don't have a credible and properly detailed plan.

Your ability to evaluate progress on your project, calculate your variance from plan, and predict the future depends on a number of key process elements. Among these elements are:

- A baseline of measurement
- Processes and methods for gathering data
- An ability to get good data
- Timeliness in reporting
- Processes, tools, and methods for analyzing past, present, and future performance

Let's examine these elements.

Establishing a Baseline of Measurement

The baseline of measurement is actually represented by your Integrated Project Plan. This includes your control schedule, project budget, and any design or performance specifications related to project deliverables. The estimates embodied in the project plan create the basis from which variance is calculated.

The fact that the baseline is an estimate, however, poses a problem with regard to maintaining control. What if an estimate is wrong? What if an element of your baseline is a poor representation of what's actually achievable?

When you encounter a variance, it can sometimes be difficult to know whether it's because of the estimator or because of the task performer. This is one of the greatest difficulties in maintaining proper control. Knowing the source of the variance is important. If you're able to distinguish an estimating problem from a performance problem, you're in a better position to take the appropriate corrective action. Unless you uncover specific estimating errors, however, assume that your baseline is reasonably accurate and use it as your basis for measuring variance and taking corrective action.

What Information Do You Need?

Exactly what kind of information should you gather to evaluate your current variance and maintain control of your project? Project analysis comprises elements of the past, present, and future. Below are listed the specific pieces of information you should request.

Schedule

- Date that each completed activity was scheduled to start and finish
- Date that each completed activity actually started and finished
- Anticipated start date of each activity
- Actual start date of each activity currently under way
- Originally scheduled completion date of each activity currently under way
- Estimated completion date of each activity currently under way
- Description of the progress made on each activity currently under way

Cost

- Estimated expenditure (or labor hours) for all activities
- Actual expenditure (or labor hours logged) for each completed activity
- Amount spent to date (or labor hours logged) on each activity currently under way
- Estimated cost to complete (or additional labor hours required) for each activity currently under way

Functionality

- Original estimation of the capabilities of final deliverables
- Current prediction of what those capabilities will be

Quality

- Original estimation of how well final deliverables will function
- Current prediction of how well they will function.

How Do You Gather Information?

Obviously, you have to gather a lot of information and keep track of many things throughout the project lifetime. How do you uncover this kind of information? What processes and methods can you use? Among the most common ones are:

Team meetings. The main conduit of current information is ordinarily your project team status meetings. As mentioned earlier, project team meetings should be conducted regularly throughout the project.

The first order of business is past performance—recording actual results of completed activities.

The second order of business is a thorough review and analysis of the condition of each activity currently under way. Since this is the main focus of most team meetings, here's a trick that can ease your life: optimum team meeting efficiency occurs (and Figure 11-1 illustrates) when the frequency of scheduled team meetings matches the average duration of scheduled activities. Applying the 4 percent rule (which we discussed in Chapter 5) to both activity duration and team meeting frequency tends to minimize the amount of time spent reporting on the status of activities currently under way (trust me, this is how the arithmetic works!).

The third order of business is to keep your eye on the future by asking for information on the predicted outcome of each activity. (We discuss this aspect later in this chapter.)

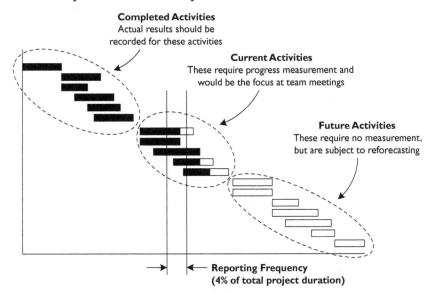

Figure 11-1. Choosing meeting frequency

Forms and templates. A number of methods exist for gathering information. Among the most straightforward, reliable methods is to provide

FOCUS ON THE REASONS AND BENEFITS
Designing and using forms and templates to gather information from your team helps you do your job. But whenever you ask people to do something that looks like additional work (such as regularly filling out data input forms), you must help them understand why you're asking them to do it and what you're going to do with their information. Even more important, tell them how this approach will make their life easier, as you will be less likely to pester them with clarifying questions later. If you fail to take these steps, team members may view your request as busywork and are likely to resist or ignore this process.

your team members with fill-in-the-blank forms and templates. If the forms and templates are designed properly, they should make life easier for team members and help to ensure that you get the type of information you need—in the form you need it—to maintain control.

Consider adapting your WBS to capture project information such as labor hours spent, current status, forecasted values, issues or problems, re-estimates of duration and cost, and so on. You could also provide copies of the project schedule that team members can mark up as appropriate to provide current status information. There are various possibilities for enabling your team members to give you information. Whatever you choose, make sure that your motives focus on making your life (and theirs) easier.

MBWA. Management by walking around (MBWA) may seem like a cliché, but it's vital for effective project leadership. Maintaining control is often more than recording information. It's assessing the motivational level of your team members, evaluating or confirming the accuracy or validity of the information you receive, and uncovering problems or issues that may not surface in a team setting. Sometimes these things can be evaluated only by spending time with team members, one-on-one. By doing this, you may be surprised at what you learn.

Software and systems support. The information management component of gathering information varies widely from one organization to the next. On some projects, project control documentation may be effectively managed with pen and paper. Others may use sophisticated, companywide mainframe systems. The amount of software and systems

The Value of Informal Communication Methods

TRICKS OF THE TRADE

Savvy project managers have discovered that information gathered through informal channels of communication can often be of more value than information gathered through more formal methods, such as team meetings. There are at least two reasons for this. First, some team members may be reluctant to reveal sensitive information in front of the entire team. Second, a project manager who spends time with individual team members demonstrates concern and is likely to promote a healthier and more open relationship with each team member. Strive to provide team members with opportunities to communicate with you and transfer information informally. It's easy to do: visit their cube (or desk), ask them to join you in a cup of coffee, or stop and chat for moment when you bump into them at the water cooler.

support you use for your projects depends on various factors, some of which we examined in Chapter 9 when discussing the amount of planning you should do regarding:

- Project complexity
- Project size
- Organizational expectations
- Organizational support (i.e., what the organization provides for you)

Many project managers find themselves somewhere in the middle of the continuum of software and systems support. They use one of the many stand-alone software packages, most of which have a respectable amount of processing capability, but still require manual data entry.

Making Sure You Get Good Information

To evaluate your position and maintain control, it's not enough to simply gather information. What you need is high-quality information. But what does *high-quality* mean? The information you need should be:

In the appropriate form. This means the information is expressed in a way that allows you to process it with relative ease. How do you ensure that you get information in a usable form? First, make your expectations clear regarding the way the information should be presented. Second, provide the forms and templates that team members can simply fill in.

Timely. Your ability to react to problems in a timely manner depends on the "freshness" of the information you receive. Since most of that information comes from team meetings, it follows that meeting frequency is critical. As mentioned earlier, I recommend a team meeting interval of about 4 percent. In other words, a reasonable frequency for a six-month project would be once per week; for an 18-month project it would be enough to meet once every three weeks, unless there were special circumstances that dictated more frequent meetings. The practice of MBWA described above also helps you receive fresh information.

Precise. We've sat in many team meetings and observed project managers attempting to ascertain the status of current activities. The responses sound like this: "I'm doing OK," "I'm on schedule," "I'm about half done," "I have a little bit more to do and then I'll be done." Needless to say, updates like these do not provide the project manager with enough information to do his or her job. Refer to the section in this chapter entitled "What Information Do You Need?" Note that these items request specific dates, durations, and dollar amounts. You need this type of specific information to maintain proper control.

Credible. The credibility of the information you receive is more closely tied to human nature than administrative processes and methods. There is often a correlation between the information validity you receive from team members and the quality of your relationship with them. The issue often revolves around how comfortable a given team member feels in giving you honest and accurate information—particularly when things aren't going well.

This comfort level is closely tied to the climate you create and the tone you set—in particular, how you react to bad news (unfavorable status reports). Figure 11-2 lists some dos and don'ts for setting up an open, honest, and credible information flow between you and your team members so you get quality information from them.

Analyzing the Information

As mentioned above, your analysis should deal primarily with schedule, cost, functionality, and quality. Let's take a closer look at how to process and interpret the information you receive—and analyze your position— in each of these areas.

- **Do** reward people for following appropriate processes, even if their results are not always favorable.
- **Don't** punish the messenger of unfavorable information, even if the messenger is responsible.
- **Do** encourage and support an "early warning" mentality in reporting.
- **Don't** spend any time placing blame when poor results are reported.
- **Do** immediately move into a mode of collaborative problem solving when problems surface.
- **Don't** ever play one team member against another, or criticize one team member while talking to another.
- **Do** demonstrate personal commitment and accountability.

Figure 11-2. Project management do's and don'ts

Analyzing the Schedule

Schedule analysis relies heavily on graphic techniques. Let's look at how schedule analysis is done. Figure 11-3 shows a basic Project Control Schedule and illustrates the four dimensions of a good Project Control Schedule: the original baseline plan, the amount of progress made, the forecasted time-to-complete, and the location of the critical path.

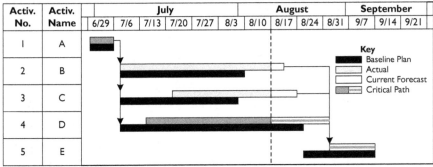

Today's Date
(Date of team meeting)

Figure 11-3. The four dimensions of a Project Control Schedule

Figure 11-4 displays the type of information that project team members might report to you in team meetings and that you would use to keep the project on schedule. Note that these inputs predict the future (called *forecast data*). As we discussed previously, your primary focus should be on the project completion date—that's why forecasts are so important.

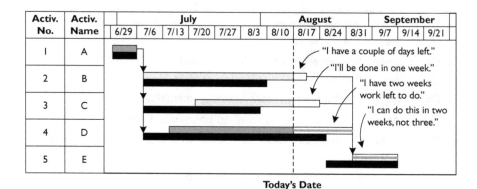

Figure 11-4. Use forecast data to maintain an accurate control schedule

Once you've gathered inputs from team members, you're ready to interpret the schedule. Interpreting the schedule in Figure 11-4 allows us to make several observations about the past performance and current status of the individual activities shown on this control schedule. For example:

- Activity A started and finished on time.
- Activity B started on time and will take much longer than expected.
- Activity C started two weeks late, but its duration hasn't changed.
- Activity D started about a week late, and its duration hasn't changed.
- Activity E is scheduled to start as soon as Activity D is completed and will take a week less to complete than originally estimated.

We can also make some observations about the overall project. Applying the critical path concept discussed in Chapter 9, we're able to see that, although Activities B, C, and D are running late, they are expected to be completed before they impact Activity E. Only Activity D seems to present a problem, as it's causing Activity E to start later than planned. This makes it a critical path activity. However, by comparing the baseline and forecast data for Activity E (the last activity in the project), we can see that the combination of all variances equals zero. In other words, we expect to finish on time. Remember that the validity of these inputs is tied to source credibility, so don't be afraid to ask questions when you see forecasts that don't make sense.

Analyzing Costs

In the past, classic cost analysis relied on charting the actual project expenditure against the anticipated project expenditure. The result would be a graph similar to the one shown in Figure 11-5.

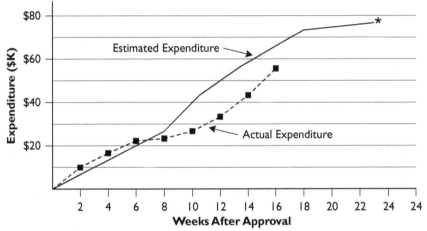

Figure 11-5. Classic cost analysis

Although this technique seems to provide a good snapshot of your current cost position, it doesn't provide detail at the activity level. This creates a challenge for you, as you can't determine which activities (if any) are of greatest concern.

You can analyze your cost position at the activity level in a manner similar to schedule analysis, where you examine the past, present, and future to determine your end point (Figure 11-6).

Figure 11-6 illustrates a cost analysis spreadsheet. For each activity, information is tracked for the baseline estimate, the amount of money spent to date, and the anticipated future expenditure. Comparing the forecasted total with the original estimate yields a calculated variance for each activity.

Project Apex Cost Summary
(Actual costs through xx/xx/xx)

Task ID	Baseline Estimate	Spent to Date	Cost to Complete	Revised Forecast	Under (Over)
001	$20,000	$4,250	$16,100	$20,350	$(350)
002	$6,700	$1,150	$5,700	$6,850	$(150)
003	$3,900	$700	$2,900	$3,600	$300
004	$14,600	$10,330	$4,050	$14,380	$220
005	$3,000	$0	$3,000	$3,000	$0
006	$4,200	$2,100	$1,900	$4,000	$200
007	$13,300	$13,500	$1,300	$14,800	$(1,500)
008	$11,500	$2,300	$8,800	$11,100	$400
Total	$77,200	$34,330	$43,750	$78,080	$(880)

Figure 11-6. Analyzing your cost position

Determining the actual expenditure to date for each activity is challenging if you don't have good labor-charging systems support. Some project managers who find themselves in this situation track the effort or resources by manually logging labor hours into a cost and schedule management software tool. Although this allows them to track costs, it's a labor-intensive process.

While developing a cost analysis spreadsheet like the one in Figure 11-6 enables you to examine costs at the activity level, it does not provide an integrated approach. In other words, it's not tied to accomplishment. While it tells you how much you've spent (cash flow), it doesn't tell you what you've gotten for your money (value). This concern can be addressed by applying the Earned Value concept.

An Integrated Approach to Analyzing Schedule and Costs: The Earned Value Concept

While performing a separate analysis of schedule and cost can certainly be helpful, it doesn't always provide an entirely accurate or comprehensive picture of project status. A better picture emerges when you integrate project effort with project cash flow. To illustrate this point, take another look at Figure 11-5. It appears as if we're under budget by about

10 percent. Good news, right?

What if we told you that the project is nearing completion. Good news becomes great news: we're nearly done and we've spent only about three-quarters of what's budgeted!

Now imagine that you were just told that the team has only completed about half of all the project work. This would be a very bad situation.

Here's how that works (referring to Figure 11-5): if you imagine that the team is half done, that's the equivalent to being back at week 12 on the timeline. Now, if you shift the current expenditure point to the left until it's directly over week 12, the result is that you're actually about 10 percent over the budget!

In each scenario, the money we've spent is identical. What's different? The amount of work that's been done.

That's where the *earned value concept* is useful. It integrates schedule with cost. There are a number of formulas associated with earned value techniques. Many books address the topic of earned value in detail. For our purposes we stay at the conceptual level.

At the core of the earned value technique are these three basic measurement components (defined below):

1. Planned Value, or PV (formerly called the Budgeted Cost of Work Scheduled)
2. Earned Value, or EV (formerly called the Budgeted Cost of Work Performed)
3. Actual Cost, or AC (formerly called the Actual Cost of Work Performed)

Note that I threw in the former names of these three components; some project managers still use these terms, as they find them to be more descriptive than the currently accepted terms.

Planned Value (PV) is a measure of the value of the work that you expect to accomplish as the project progresses. It's expressed in terms of money, and plots the monetary value of the individual activities that appear on the project schedule. It's equivalent to the conventional concept of the planned budget. In Figure 11-5, the Estimated Expenditure line is the Planned Value.

Earned Value (EV) is a measure of the value of what you've accomplished. It charts the cost (i.e., the value) of the work you've gotten done at any point in time. The original activity-by-activity cost estimates are used as the basis of this calculation.

Actual Cost (AC) refers to what you paid for what you've accomplished. This would be your actual expenditure at any point in time. In Figure 11-5, AC is represented by the Actual Expenditure dotted line.

And so, conceptually, your cost status can be evaluated by comparing EV to AC—in other words, what you thought you'd have to pay and what you've actually paid—for a given amount of accomplishment.

Your schedule status would be established by comparing EV against PV—what you expected to accomplish against what you actually accomplished—in terms of the expenditure estimates of the activities.

Evaluating your schedule position using earned value can be useful, but you can do the same thing by using the schedule analysis techniques described earlier in this chapter.

Even if you don't make rigorous earned value calculations, one of the most valuable by-products of earned value is the practice of evaluating schedule status through the use of *physical progressing* methods.

> **Physical progressing** A way to express accomplishment in tangible, verifiable terms. For example, one of your team members may report being "50 percent complete" on an activity.
> **KEY TERM** How can you tell? If you're using physical progressing methods, the person executing that activity would be expected to produce something (a deliverable, if possible) that will substantiate the level of accomplishment reported. By doing this, you can more accurately judge whether 50 percent is a fair evaluation of status.

You do this by breaking down an activity into smaller parts and then assessing how much progress is being made on an incremental basis. Figure 11-7 illustrates three methods for physical progressing.

Determining the best method for your project depends on the nature of the activity being measured. Using techniques such as physical progressing helps ensure that you and your team members understand progress in the same way. It also sends a message that you're measuring progress, not just recording it.

Type of Measurement	How It Works	Normal Application
Units Completed	If there were five equal tasks, finishing one equates to 20% complete, finishing two equates to 40% complete, and so forth.	Used when a major activity consists of a number of equal or nearly equal tasks, each requiring about the same amount of effort to complete.
Incremental Milestone	25% 50% 75% 100% ├──┼──┼──┼──┤	Choose arbitrary, incremental checkpoints, then determine the progress that should be made at those points.
Weighted Milestones	Spec'd Designed Built Installed ├──┼──┼──┼──┤ 20% 50% 80% 100%	Used when phases exist within a major activity. It's not necessary for milestones to be equally spaced.

Figure 11-7. Three methods for physical progressing

Analyzing Deliverable Performance (Functionality and Quality)

Analyzing the project deliverables—in particular, whether they will meet functionality and quality targets—is challenging. In some cases, the existence of a deliverable cannot be verified until it's completed.

And keep in mind that one of your primary objectives is to keep deliverable performance from being degraded. It's important to note that deliverable performance can fall short for two reasons.

1. **Deliverables fail to perform as expected.** It's possible to create deliverables that are made according to design or specification, but don't turn out as well as expected. Perhaps they don't perform as anticipated or they can't fully accomplish their intended purpose. This kind of outcome is not uncommon in situations where you're creating something new, where significant research and development are required. If you think this could happen on your project, make sure the customer for the deliverables is fully aware that performance problems are a possibility.

2. **Performance standards are altered during the project.** Sometimes a decision is made during the project to lower the project deliverables' performance standards. This situation can occur if it's determined that what was thought to be achievable simply isn't. In other cases, standards are lowered to compensate for cost or schedule problems.

From a management standpoint, the difference between these two situations is huge. An inability to meet performance standards because of technological challenges is often understandable. If handled properly—that is, with the customer's understanding and cooperation—this situation shouldn't reflect on your management ability. However, if you or a member of your team trade off deliverable performance as a way to save time or money—without the express permission of the client—you're asking for trouble. Make sure that you review with your customer any contemplated modifications to performance standards. And make sure that team members understand that this is never their decision to make alone.

How Should You React to the Information?

OK, you've gathered information and done some analysis. Now it's time to react.

If everything is going well, little reaction is necessary. Most of the time, any action you might be inclined to take would be in response to an undesirable situation. This is commonly known as taking *corrective action.*

KEY TERM **Corrective action** Measures taken to get a project back on course. It typically pertains to action taken to remedy an unfavorable set of circumstances (schedule delay, cost overrun, or deliverable performance issue).

When steering a ship, knowing what to do to get back on course isn't complicated. Not so with project work. You've got people, processes, and technology to worry about. You're dealing with interdependent dimensions (cost, schedule, functionality, and quality). And there may be many strategies for getting your project headed in the right direction.

There is no right way to take corrective action. Choosing the best course of action is situational; you must carefully consider many factors, including the following.

Know when to take action. This is one of the most difficult aspects of corrective action. There's an adage: "A project slips one day at a time." Does that mean you should take action as soon as your project falls one day behind? Probably not. But it does suggest that you shouldn't ignore the situation. Early detection is critical to keeping your project from straying too far off course. This is one reason that regular team meetings are so valuable.

Keep a sharp and watchful eye on a situation—and make sure that team members know you're watching it. Sometimes a simple nudge in the form of a reminder (e.g., "Don't forget you're supposed to be done in two weeks") is all that's required if an issue is detected early enough. The worst thing you can do is ignore a situation, believing that somehow the team will make up the lost time by the end of the project. This won't happen unless you make it happen. Problems rarely work themselves out; you must take action to fix them.

Decide whether to fix the problem (immediate action) or compensate for it (future action). When a problem occurs, we're often tempted to fix it immediately. However, in some situations, this may not be the correct thing to do.

In some cases, your best course of action may be to accommodate the present situation and try to counteract the effects of the problem through future actions. If you choose to address the problem through future

---

BRAD LEARNS A LESSON

FOR EXAMPLE

In one of the project team meetings, Carol reports that software coding is falling behind.

"It's more difficult than I'd originally envisioned," she says as she gives Brad the bad news.

"That activity is supposed to be completed by the end of the month, you know," Brad notes, checking the schedule. "I'll see if I can get you some help, Carol." He moves on to the next agenda item before Carol can respond.

The next day, Brad gets a temporary programmer assigned and feels confident that he's resolved the problem.

In the next team meeting, Carol reports that she's fallen even farther behind.

That's a surprise for Brad. "What about the programmer I got for you?"

"Sorry, Brad," Carol says. "It took several days just to orient him to Project Apex and what we're trying to do with this program. He only just started being productive a few days ago."

"Well, just finish up as soon as you can," Brad says, having learned a valuable lesson about "throwing bodies at problems."

action, be sure to keep everyone informed and to modify the project plan to reflect your intentions.

Avoid the micromanagement pitfall. If you're action oriented (as many project managers are), you may be tempted to personally jump into any and all problems. You may justify your action by saying, "I'll get involved only long enough to get the problem under control. Then I'll back off."

Avoid this temptation, except possibly in serious or extreme situations. First, you won't have enough time to jump into every problem that surfaces. Second—and more important—you'll cause your team members to resent your interventions. By getting personally involved, you're sending a message that you don't trust team members to resolve problems on their own.

Your best course of action is to remind them of the need to correct the problem or suggest a remedy and, if needed, offer yourself as a support resource. This demonstrates trust and frees you to spend your time managing issues pertaining to the overall project.

Choose the best recovery strategy. Many courses of action are open to you to recover from difficulties and try to ensure that the team meets critical project targets. Among your basic options are those listed below, not in any particular order except for the first and last options.

- **Push for compliance.** In most cases, your first course of action should be to maintain the original plan. In other words, don't assume that you should automatically accept or accommodate the contemplated changes. Sometimes a firm reminder of the commitment and an offer of support is enough to stimulate better performance.

- **Recover in later tasks.** This is often a better option than attempting to fix the immediate problem. Be sure that future plans are reflected in the project schedule.

- **Add resources.** Get additional help. Be sure to consider the potential increase in expenditure and the possibility of diminishing returns when resources are added. Having three times the resources on an activity doesn't necessarily mean it will be completed in one-third the time.

- **Accept substitutions.** When something is unavailable or expected to be delivered late, substitute a comparable item. Consider the potential effects on deliverable performance.

- **Use alternative work methods.** Sometimes you can find a more expedient way to accomplish the work. However, changing work methods often has an effect on cost and/or schedule.
- **Accept partial deliverables.** When it makes sense, accepting delivery of the items you need in "batches" may allow you to keep the project moving forward.
- **Offer incentives.** Offer a bonus or other inducement to improve performance. This strategy is often directed at suppliers. Penalty clauses may have the same effect, but are a negative strategy.
- **Renegotiate cost and schedule targets.** Explore the possibility of extending the deadline or increasing the budget, if it helps. This will probably be easier if you can show that problems are due to estimating errors rather than performance issues.
- **Reduce scope.** Reduce the quality and/or performance requirements of the project deliverables to reduce the work necessary. This should ordinarily be your last course of action, when maintaining cost or schedule targets is paramount. It's imperative that all stakeholders agree before you take this course of action.
- **Understand trade-offs.** As mentioned earlier, the dimensions of schedule, cost, functionality, and quality are interdependent. This means that taking corrective action may involve trading off one dimension for another. For example, adding resources may alleviate your schedule problems, but will probably increase costs. Using less expensive materials may save money, but could affect the functionality or quality of the project deliverables.

It follows, then, that you can't always protect the integrity of all four dimensions at once. Which dimension(s) should you favor? This is exactly the question you should ask of key stakeholders—particularly the customer—at the outset of the project. Many times, they'll have a preference.

If you're lucky, stakeholders will express their preferences: "I want you to hold the schedule, even if the costs run over" or "If you need to take more time to make sure this thing works, do it!"

Unfortunately, not all stakeholders are this explicit. However, if you spend time discussing the project with them, you'll often come to understand what their preferences are and you can confirm that with them.

TRICKS OF THE TRADE

INTERVIEWING TECHNIQUES

Determining stakeholders' priorities for schedule, cost, functionality, and performance targets is difficult at times. One method that often yields good results consists of using an interviewing approach and asking some hypothetical questions. For example, ask your customer: "What if the project were to run over by $20,000?" or "What if we ran into problems and were three weeks late?"

Take note of their answers—and their body language. This often provides you with insights about what is important to them. This enables you to make intelligent trade-offs if you need to take corrective action.

Learn from all problems. Simply resolving a problem when it occurs is not enough. One habit you should adopt is to pause to reflect on the problem you've just encountered. Ask yourself (and others) key questions, such as:

- Could this problem happen again?
- If so, can we prevent it? How?
- If we can't prevent it, can we mitigate its effects?
- Could this problem happen to others? If so, how do I alert them?
- Does this problem affect others? How? What can be done?

Taking the time to reflect on problems may help you and others in your organization learn from your experiences.

Execution and Control Documents

During the third project phase, the *Execution Phase*, the prescribed work is performed. As project manager, you continuously monitor progress, and you make and record appropriate adjustments as variances from the original plan. Throughout this phase, the project team remains focused on meeting the objectives developed at the project outset.

Figure 11-8 illustrates the key documents you should create as part of project execution and control.

Purchasing and Contracting Documents

You'll likely have to procure materials and labor on your project. The key documents associated with this process include:

- **Material listing:** Description of materials to be purchased.
- **Purchase order (PO):** Form used to place orders for materials with outside suppliers.

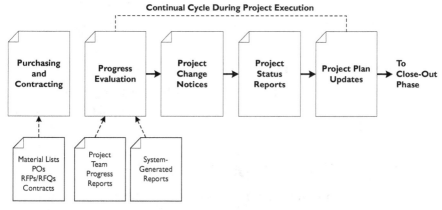

Figure 11-8. Key documents in the Process Execution phase

- **Request for proposal/request for quote (RFP/RFQ):** Documents used to solicit proposals from prospective vendors of products or services.
- **Contracts:** Legally binding agreements with external suppliers of goods and services.

Progress Evaluation

These reports describe the amount of work being accomplished. The documents typically come from two sources:

1. **Team-generated reports:** This is the information you're collecting in your regular team meetings. You should have documents to serve as a record such as marked-up schedules or filled-in forms and templates.
2. **System-generated reports:** If your organization has the capability to store and retrieve project data, such as labor hours or material costs, download this data periodically and keep the documents in your project file.

Project Change Notice

There are many names for this critical document, which is used to document and get approval for any significant deviation from the project baseline. At the end of your project, you ought to be able to reconcile the overall deviation between where you ended up and where you told management you'd end up. That reconciliation is embodied in a stack (hopefully short!) of project change notices.

You should provide regular updates to management, whether through written reports, one-on-one meetings with the project sponsor, or periodic stand-up presentations.

Project Plan Updates

The project plan should be revised regularly to reflect any changes. As activities are completed and new information about the future becomes available, prepare new forecasts.

Manager's Checklist for Chapter 11

- ☑ Project control does not mean dictating to team members how to perform their activities or roles.

- ☑ The project control process should focus on gathering and analyzing information that will optimize decision making.

- ☑ The project manager must gather information and insight on the past, present, and future when making decisions on guiding the course of the project.

- ☑ Essential to the information-gathering process is free, open, and honest communication between the project team members and the project leader.

- ☑ Corrective action should resolve problems in a way that minimizes losses to project targets (schedule, cost, functionality, and quality) at the lowest additional risk.

- ☑ Decisions on corrective action should be influenced by stakeholder preferences. Determine which targets—schedule, cost, functionality, or quality—are most important to them.

Bringing the Project to a Successful Conclusion

Brad's first excursion into the world of project management has been going well. Sure, there were some rough spots, but all in all, Brad is proud of the job he's done. Project Apex is nearing what he hopes will be a smooth and successful conclusion.

But just when Brad thought he'd be able to kick back and watch Project Apex coast to the finish line, things began to heat up. Attendance at his team meetings has been steadily tapering off. He's having difficulty reaching some people who were trying to wrap up their last few activities. Brad has been getting questions about what the customer may be expecting, and he can't seem to get any answers.

Brad is beginning to wonder if he's losing his grip. The project plan doesn't seem to be a great deal of help now—at least compared to how much he relied on it throughout project execution. He thinks about calling his unofficial mentor, Ted. He changes his mind, though, feeling that he has probably bothered Ted enough already.

Why don't we see what kind of help *we* can give Brad.

Early Termination: Not as Bad as You Think

Before we direct our attention to Brad's current situation, let's imagine for a moment that management had cancelled Project Apex early in its life. As strange as it may sound, this is a situation that should happen more often than it does. Here's why.

In Chapters 2 and 4, we noted that the most fundamental objective of projects is to achieve positive business results and generate economic gain. Remember, projects are investments that your organization makes, from which it expects a return. In real life, we know that investments sometimes go bad. The same applies to projects. Conditions can change in such a way that a project ceases to become the strategic, operational, or financial winner that we thought it was at its beginning. It may no longer be wise to keep spending money on it and it should be terminated. Too often, however, these projects aren't terminated. Among the more common reasons are these:

Falling asleep at the wheel. You should be testing project viability—or financial justification—on a continuous basis throughout the project. Some organizations don't do this—once a project is approved, it simply moves forward until it's completed. In today's fast-paced and constantly shifting environment, it's possible that change will undermine the project's original business proposition. Be sure that someone reconsiders the economic viability of all projects periodically and terminates projects that have lost their business underpinnings.

Fear of failure. In many people's minds—and in many of the organizations we are familiar with—early project termination has somehow become linked with failure. This couldn't be further from the truth. Early project termination (for the right business reasons) is smart management; it's a process of reallocating funds from a now-poor investment to a good one.

Inertial pride. Once a project is under way, a certain amount of momentum is generated by the work that has already gone into a particular project. Pride swells, and a feeling that "we must see this thing through to the end" begins to take hold in people's minds. Even though a team (or organization) senses that a project is on shaky ground, emotional issues such as not being viewed as quitters and finishing what was started seem to become part of the determination process of whether to terminate the project. Couple these feelings with the sweat equity that's been invested,

---

THE EARLIER THE BETTER

TRICKS OF THE TRADE

Normally, there should be no shame in canceling a project that's already under way if it has lost its business justification. This determination should be made as soon as possible—particularly from the standpoint of wasted time, money, and resources. That's why you should prepare business cases and establish financial justification as early as possible in the project life cycle and revisit them frequently throughout the project's early stages.

---

and under these circumstances, the project is almost certain to continue even when it no longer makes good business sense.

Management Challenges at the End of the Project

OK, now back to Brad's situation. As the end of his project approaches, Brad finds himself facing a new set of challenges, as you undoubtedly will. These challenges will test your ability to bring the project to a successful conclusion, even if everything has been going well to date. Most of the challenges you'll face fall into one of three broad categories: technical, project team, and your customer.

Technical Challenges
- Start-up problems with new products, equipment, or facilities
- Thorough identification and agreement on all remaining deliverables
- Loss of control of the charges to the project
- Difficulties in securing useful project historical data

Project Team Challenges
- Loss of team cohesion as some members complete their work
- Loss of interest in tasks such as documentation and administrative detail
- Attention diverted as members transition to new projects or other work
- Fear of no future work, causing potential foot-dragging

Customer Challenges
- Agreement on outstanding commitments
- Absence of a clear handoff strategy

- Change of responsible personnel at critical transition points
- Unavailability of key customer advisors

Let's examine how to address these challenges by taking a closer look at the science of successful project closure, beginning with a list of the key elements of project closure.

Key Elements of Successful Project Closure

The project's closeout phase should be given as much or more project management attention than any other phase. While there may be a smaller total volume of work, it can be chaotic. Project closure requires close attention to several managerial functions. More than any other phase, closeout requires a diverse set of technical, organizational, and leadership skills. Here are the things

SMART MANAGING

THE "ART" OF PROJECT CLOSURE

Many challenges that surface at the end of your project will be rooted in behavioral issues. This will test your leadership ability. You must remain on the lookout for behavioral cues that indicate the existence of one or more challenges (remember our discussion about the "art of project management" in Chapter 1?).

that you must do well to maximize your chances for a successful project completion:

Ensure that the project delivers what was promised. This should have been tracked throughout the entire execution and control phase. As discussed in Chapter 11, you must continually monitor the functionality and quality of the project deliverables and protect them from degrading. This helps you avoid last-minute surprises.

Actively lead the project team through a confused period. The key word here is *actively*. Make your visibility greater at this time than at any other time since the beginning. Your project team may begin to disintegrate as a functional unit as it nears completion. Communication becomes more difficult, as you can no longer rely on a captive audience each week at your team meetings. Organizing people and things also becomes more difficult. These issues require that you maintain a high profile and assume a position of strong leadership.

Ensure timely completion of the "odds-and-ends" (punch list management). As mentioned previously, there comes a point when you can probably abandon the original project plan. You will find yourself scrambling to complete the remaining items. When that happens, you'll find it helpful to focus everyone's attention on the specific work items required to get the job done. You handle this through the punch list process described a bit later in this chapter.

Prepare for the transition to the next phase in the overall project life cycle. Most projects have an afterlife. The products of your project are accepted and used by a customer. Most organizations view project managers being responsible for ensuring a smooth "handoff" to the customer or user. In fact, don't be surprised if this activity requires your involvement—on a limited basis, at least—after the traditional project completion.

Secure consensus that the project has met the completion criteria. You established these criteria at the beginning of your project. If you ignore this issue until the end of your project, disagreements may become significant. Resolving certain types of problems late in the project can involve significant rework.

Obtain customer acceptance and verify customer satisfaction. This is not done enough—at least not in a formalized way. Strive to create an almost ceremonial atmosphere around customer acceptance and customer satisfaction. Just as a formal kickoff meeting communicates project initiation, a formal session where you secure customer satisfaction and acceptance should signal successful project completion in a positive and upbeat way.

Ensure that the project records reflect accurate as-built data. This refers primarily to the process of updating all the documents related to your project to reflect the project as it exists. This ensures accurate historical data, which can be of value to future project teams.

Project files (most notably the project plan) should be updated to reflect the final actual outcomes in terms of cost, schedule, functionality, and quality. Design documents and specification sheets should be updated to reflect how the deliverables actually look and perform. Contractual and procurement records should reflect any modifications to agreements or contractual exceptions.

Transfer what you've learned to others. The process of performing a lessons learned analysis is described below. Whether you perform a full-fledged analysis or simply jot a few notes, it is important and useful to transfer any critical information you've accumulated or lessons you've learned to anyone who may benefit from your recently acquired wisdom.

Acknowledge the contributions of others. Formally recognizing those who helped you achieve project success is not just a nice thing to do, it's a strong building block for the future—yours as well as the organization's. People who work hard and make significant contributions become demotivated if their work goes unrecognized, which hurts organizational effectiveness. And at a personal level, if you gain a reputation as someone who appreciates a job well done—and you show it—you're more likely to garner the resources you want on your future projects.

SMART MANAGING

SHOW THEM THAT YOU CARE

Study after study shows that the personal touch in recognition means a great deal to nearly everyone. Financial rewards are nice, but personal displays of appreciation are considered more meaningful. A personal affirmation tells people that their contribution made a difference. A simple note or heartfelt "thank you" can be a powerful motivator.

Bring the project to efficient administrative closure. This may include a wide range of issues. For example, you need to address accounting issues, such as closing charge account numbers. It also includes ensuring that all outstanding invoices have been submitted and paid. It may also include closing out rental or lease agreements, as well as disposing of or storing leftover materials.

A Few More Words About Punch List Management

For me, the value and importance of effective punch list management became apparent through a personal experience with a home builder a few years ago. As my house neared completion, it became painfully obvious that there were a number of odds and ends that needed to be done before I (the customer) would consider the project successfully completed. The pain stemmed from the fact that my builder was not taking command of the situation and driving these few items to completion. Time was passing with little progress. My satisfaction level deteriorated on a daily basis—despite the fact that the project had gone well up to that point. A friend suggested that I create a punch list of activities and present it to the builder, suggesting that he get these things taken care of immediately. It worked.

The punch list concept is readily transferable to any kind of project. In fact, you are likely to reach a point on most of your projects where only a few action items stand between you and successful project completion. These action items may not have been included on your original project plan. This is because loose ends and unexpected issues often accompany a project's waning days.

In situations like this, it can be helpful to adopt a more directive management style. Developing a punch list of outstanding action items, reviewing it with all key stakeholders (most notably the customer), and creating a miniplan around the punch list is an effective strategy for driving your project to a rapid, organized, and successful conclusion.

Figure 12-1 illustrates the process for punch list project management. You will undoubtedly notice that this approach is a scaled-down version of the planning process introduced earlier in this book.

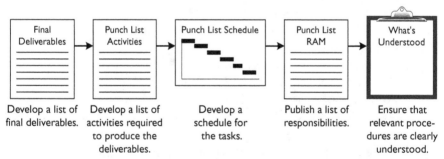

Figure 12-1. Punch list project management

Punch list project management The process of managing all the little things that pop up at the end of a project that must be done before declaring the project successfully completed. There are nearly always such items, often unanticipated, so it's good to be ready and to know how to handle them, whatever they are. **KEY TERM**

Developing a Project Completion Checklist

The punch list focuses directly on delivery of the main project deliverables. However, you must also be concerned with many other functions involved in project closure. These include many often-overlooked aspects of project delivery as well as the completion of organizational items. To preclude things from being overlooked, develop a *Project Completion Checklist*.

PROJECT COMPLETION CHECKLIST

Customer Issues
- ❑ Complete all deliverables
- ❑ Install and test deliverables
- ❑ Prepare operating manual
- ❑ Prepare maintenance manual
- ❑ Train customer's personnel
- ❑ Agree on level of follow-up support
- ❑ Conduct formal acceptance review with customer
- ❑ Verify customer satisfaction

TOOLS

Organizational Issues
- ❑ Summarize learnings; communicate to the organization
- ❑ Prepare final technical reports
- ❑ Evaluate project performance
- ❑ Conduct final review with management
- ❑ Prepare project historical files and place in archive

Personnel Issues
- ❑ Recognize/reward team performance
- ❑ Write performance evaluations for project team
- ❑ Assist in reassignment of project personnel

Administrative/Other Issues
- ❑ Dispose of leftover project material
- ❑ Close down temporary site operations
- ❑ Submit final invoices
- ❑ Forward all final payments
- ❑ Close out project charge codes and work orders

Transferring What You've Learned to Others

One way to support the ongoing improvement of your organization's project execution methods comes in the form of Lessons Learned Studies. The purpose of a *Lessons Learned Study* is to obtain information through the systematic review of project experiences. Understanding the nature of positive and negative experiences allows future projects to avoid unfavorable influences (problems) and exploit favorable opportunities.

Include input from all key stakeholders in your study, with you and the project team typically taking a leading role in organizing and carrying out the study. The format and structure of your lessons learned sessions (i.e., the logistics) will vary, but the sessions are often done in a team meeting context, using an approach similar to brainstorming.

The Lessons Learned Process

You will probably find the lessons learned process to be most productive when it is oriented toward identifying challenges encountered during the project and suggesting ways to avoid similar problems on future projects. You accomplish this by asking the following questions for each identified problem:

What was the problem and its impact? Get a description of the perceived problem and its specific effect(s) on the project. Find out what happened to the project as a result of the problem.

What caused this problem to occur? Find out the known or perceived root cause of the problem. If unknown, the cost of securing this knowledge needs to be weighed against its potential benefit.

Why was the problem undetected? This involves a search for flaws in monitoring, control, or reporting methods. Caution: This question can be sensitive, as it may involve individual performance problems.

> **Root cause** The fundamental cause of a problem in a process. Usually a problem occurs in a process **KEY TERM** because something went wrong in the immediately preceding step(s). However, this is the not the root cause. The root cause may have been something that happened much earlier and caused a chain reaction that resulted in the problem you're now addressing. Look for the root cause if you want to eliminate the problem permanently.

Can this problem be avoided in the future? Here you're asking for suggestions on specific steps aimed at precluding a future occurrence. Total elimination is not always possible; however, you may be able to develop

BE SENSITIVE

Inquiring about the cause of certain problems may present a challenge if done in a team setting. An individual performance issue, such as neglect, inattention, ignorance, or incompetence may have caused the problem. Anticipate and avoid situations where personal embarrassment can occur. Providing an outlet for anonymous input is a good way to reduce the chances of surfacing sensitive issues in front of the entire group.

strategies that reduce the probability that it will happen again.

If it cannot be avoided, are there ways it could be detected? Here you're looking for suggestions on how the team can alter monitoring, control, or reporting methods in ways that allow for earlier or more reliable problem detection.

Tips on Conducting Effective Lessons Learned Studies

In addition to following the process steps outlined above, consider these tips for ensuring a satisfying experience for everyone involved:

Don't wait until the end of the project to solicit input. Waiting until the last minute to conduct lessons learned studies can be problematic. Your team may have partially dissolved, making it difficult to get everyone together. Even if you do get them together, the enthusiasm level won't be what you'd like. Finally, it can be taxing on the memories of those involved, and you may get input that's been altered by the passage of time. Conduct lessons learned sessions periodically—either at the end of a logical phase of the project or at some regular interval of team meetings.

Allow the opportunity for submitting input anonymously. As mentioned above, this may allow information and ideas to reach you that are unlikely to surface in group sessions or would be inappropriate to raise publically.

Maintain up-to-date, accurate records. This reduces reliance on people's memories. It also facilitates the process of determining root causes, verifying the extent of problems, correlating possible causes and effects, etc.

Examine successes as well as problems. Reviewing positive effects can reinforce the value of certain methods or processes, particularly those that people tend to avoid or undervalue.

Tips on Getting Others to Implement Your Lessons

It's one thing to alert others to the problems you encountered and to provide information about what you and your team have encountered. However, if you do not structure your information in a way that others can apply the lessons you've learned, your organization hasn't really benefited. Below are some suggestions to ensure that your wisdom is acted on:

Don't relate lessons learned only to the specific context of your project. Make sure you express lessons learned in general terms to benefit the organization at large. Generalize the conclusions from your project's lessons learned in a way that's meaningful to the widest possible audience.

Don't only communicate what went well and what didn't go well. Unfortunately, some lessons learned studies are little more than a brain dump of what went well and what didn't go well. A lack of analysis—or synthesis—fails to provide others in the organization with a meaningful lesson. For others to benefit, they need to know how to avoid the problem(s) or to reduce the impact if the problem(s) occur.

Include lessons learned reviews as a front-end activity in the project life cycle. Lessons learned studies are traditionally thought of as concluding activities only. This one-dimensional view fails to ensure their application by future project teams. Some organizations have addressed this problem by including a step near the beginning of their project process that obligates project teams to review lessons learned files as part of their up-front planning. This strategy "closes the loop" on the learning cycle and helps to ensure that the team applies these lessons.

Closeout Documents

During the *Project Closeout Phase*, the emphasis is on verifying that the project has satisfied (or is expected to satisfy) the original need. Ideally, the project culminates with a smooth transition from *deliverable creation* (the project) to *deliverable utilization* (the postproject life cycle); that is, the project customer accepts and uses the deliverables. Throughout this phase, project resources (the members of the project team) are gradually redeployed. Finally, the project shuts down.

Punch list management. As mentioned in Chapter 11, near the end of your project you're likely to recognize that there are a number of tasks to be

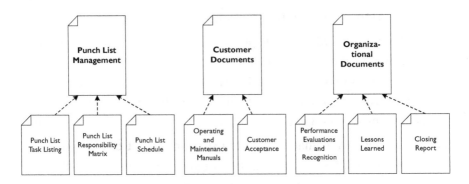

Figure 12-2. Key documents of the project close-out phase

completed to bring your project to a successful conclusion. This process is called *punch list management,* as we discussed in the previous chapter. It may make sense to create a small plan around the punch list items that would include these documents:

- **Punch List Task Listing:** A list of the tasks remaining that you should review with your customer
- **Punch List Responsibility Matrix:** A smaller version of the Responsibility Assignment Matrix, showing who's responsible for executing the punch list tasks
- **Punch List Schedule:** A schedule that includes only the items on the punch list, which you should review with your customer to avoid surprises

Customer documentation. The key documents related to handing off the project and project deliverables to the customer include:

- **Operating and maintenance manuals:** If your deliverables include equipment that the customer or user is to place into service, you should provide information on how to operate and/or maintain the equipment as part of the original project agreement.
- **Customer acceptance:** This is a critical document. You should always confirm that the customer is satisfied, ready, and willing to accept the deliverables of the project and that the customer considers the project formally concluded.

Organizational documents. There are a few key documents that are of interest to your organization at the end of the project, including:

> **THINK OF DOCUMENTATION AT THE BEGINNING!**
> All too often, operating, maintenance, service, and other manuals are not considered until the end of the project. This unanticipated work may create an unforeseen expense or a schedule delay. Think about these kinds of documents at the beginning of your project—when you're planning and estimating the project.

- **Performance evaluations and recognition:** You may be asked by the resource (departmental) providers to write evaluative reports on team members' performance. Use this opportunity to formally recognize the efforts of individual team members. However, it's often of more value to create separate documents that can be placed in team members' permanent records.

- **Lessons learned:** This is a technique to transfer the knowledge gained through your project experiences to the rest of your organization. The document can take many forms, but it's often a written report that gets circulated across the entire organization.

- **Closing report:** Some organizations require a formal report that describes how well the project met its original targets, explains deviations from the plan, and tells whether the benefits promised in the original business case are likely to be realized. For technology-rich projects, the organization often expects technical reports that describe the project team's experiences in using or creating the technology.

And So We've Reached the End

Or should we say that Brad has reached the end? When all is said and done, Brad has done a fine job of managing Project Apex. Through his experiences, he has learned a tremendous amount about project management. He has learned that having a well-designed, well-documented project management process is essential if his organization is to continue to benefit from the projects it pursues.

Brad has learned many valuable lessons about the benefits of planning.

And he has learned that projects are really small investments that his organization makes, making projects like a business enterprise—something he had never fully appreciated as a technical contributor. He has come to appreciate the role that his management plays, and how important the organization's support is to project success.

He's found out that risk and uncertainty aren't too intimidating, as long as you have a process for dealing with them. In fact, he's learned that nearly everything he did that related to project management was supported by a sound process—including communication and documentation!

He has learned that life as a project manager is all about getting things done through others—a radical departure from his previous job duties. Brad has learned that being a project manager is a surprisingly demanding job, but a job that has been very rewarding for him, nonetheless.

"I'd really like to do this again," Brad says to himself, just as his phone rings. He picks it up before the second ring. It's his boss, Gina.

"Brad, I'd like you to stop by my office right after lunch today," says the voice on the other end of the line.

Brad smiles as he unwraps his sandwich. This time he'll know what to expect.

Manager's Checklist for Chapter 12

☑ Early termination of a project—as long as it's done for the right business reasons—should be viewed as a success, not a failure.

☑ Several unique issues and challenges are likely to surface at the end of projects. Some you can anticipate and plan for—many you cannot.

☑ Treat the last few activities that have to get done as a separate, small project. Plan and schedule them, then aggressively drive them to completion. Failure to complete the project in a timely fashion can significantly impact the customer's perception of satisfaction and success.

☑ Transfer everything you've learned to others within your organization who may benefit from your experiences—good or bad.

☑ Good luck in your future project management endeavors!

Index

Index

V

Validity of estimates, 80
Visits, informal, 47
Voice mail, 46
Voice of the Customer analysis, 109

W

Weighted Factor Scoring Matrix,
 62–63, 95–97
Work Breakdown Structures

creating, 152–156
dimensions of work, 157–158
rationale for, 156–157, 177
schedule activities from, 161
use in cost management, 173
Worker involvement in planning,
 72–73
Work packages, defined, 152
Work statements, 100–101, 110
Written communication, 44

About the Author

Gary R. Heerkens, PMP, CPM, MPM, CIPM, CPC, MMC, CBM, CIPA, PEng, MBA is the president of Management Solutions Group, a firm that provides progressive and effective project management training and consulting solutions. Before establishing Management Solutions Group, he managed projects for Eastman Kodak for over 20 years and later served as staff assistant to Kodak's director of project management, developing and delivering project management training, developing project process methodology, and consulting within Kodak.

Mr. Heerkens is a long-standing seminar provider for Project Management Institute's SeminarsWorld series, and is the project management education provider for the Purchasing Management Association of Canada. He has been invited to speak at nearly every PMI Global Congress since 1998—including encore requests in 2007 and 2008.

Mr. Heerkens is a contributing editor to PMI's *PM Network* magazine, writing on "the business of projects." In addition to this book, he authored *The Business-Savvy Project Manager*, published in 2006.

Mr. Heerkens is an active member of several professional societies, including PMI, IAPPM, APBM, AAPM, and IPMA, where he has received a number of professional certifications; he has been honored as a Fellow by IAPPM and by AAPM. He was president of the PMI Rochester Chapter from 1998-2001, and was reelected president in 2005-2006. He's a licensed Professional Engineer in New York and holds an MBA from RIT.

You can reach Gary via his company's website, www.4msginc.com.

9 780071 818483